THE CHICKEN COOKBOOK

THE CHICKEN COOKBOOK

by Anne Chamberlain

LONDON
W FOULSHAM & CO LTD
New York   Toronto   Cape Town   Sydney

W Foulsham & Co Ltd
Yeovil Road, Slough, Berks, England

ISBN 0–572–00978–x

© W Foulsham & Co Ltd 1977

Typeset, printed and bound
in Great Britain by
REDWOOD BURN LIMITED
Trowbridge & Esher

CONTENTS

Chapter One

ALL ABOUT CHICKEN

Chicken is a wonderfully versatile food, and we can use it in dozens of different ways in our kitchens. Not so long ago, a chicken was an expensive luxury and was usually served traditionally roasted as a very special Sunday meal. Now modern breeding methods have produced birds which compare favourably in price with other meat. Small birds are available for small families, and chicken joints can be easily purchased to make a meal for one or two people, or for a whole crowd.

In spite of lower prices, chicken still has an air of luxury because it goes so well with many other tasty ingredients. A few mushrooms, a pinch of fresh herbs, a spoonful of wine or cream can produce a gourmet meal. On the other hand, a chicken prepared with root vegetables and rich gravy makes a satisfying and delicious meal for a hungry family.

The recipes in this book specify a bird of average weight, i.e. 3 lb/1.5 kg, as this size is obtainable in most shops and freezer centres. For a larger family, a 4–5 lb/2–2.5 kg chicken will produce a main meal, and the leftovers will make a second-day dish, with possibly soup and sandwiches as well. When chicken joints are used, four will feed the average family, but recipes may be easily halved or doubled according to the size of the meal. Small 3 lb/1.5 kg chickens may be easily jointed at home with a heavy sharp knife cleaving the breastbone, then dividing each half into two pieces. Individual chicken breasts, drumsticks and wings are often obtainable.

If a frozen bird is used, it is most important that either a whole bird or joints must be completely thawed before cooking. Thaw it slowly in the refrigerator, still in the wrappings, and be sure to remove the giblets before cooking the bird. These giblets may be simmered in water to produce stock for the recipe or for gravy, or the stock can be used later for soup. If stock is not available, as when joints are purchased, use a chicken stock cube dissolved in hot water.

A good chicken deserves good carving. Use a really sharp knife, and carve first one side, then the other. Remove the whole leg from the bird and divide it into two portions. Slice the breast vertically off the carcass, making each slice long enough to include some stuffing. Finally, take off the wing and thigh together and serve whole.

When the main meal is over, remove all remaining chicken flesh from the carcass and store it in the refrigerator for another meal. Break up the carcass and simmer it in water with an onion, carrot, herbs and seasoning, to make good stock which can be used for other dishes or for soup.

Chapter Two

ROAST CHICKEN

A whole chicken may be roasted very simply with herbs and seasoning for flavouring and just a little oil or butter for basting. Most people enjoy a stuffed chicken, so try traditional parsley-and-thyme stuffing or experiment with a fruit, bacon or sweet-corn stuffing. Stuff a bird very lightly or the stuffing becomes solid and unappetizing during cooking. Roast a chicken in a moderate oven and allow about 20 minutes longer for a stuffed bird than for an unstuffed one. Traditional accompaniments for a chicken include clear gravy, bread sauce, bacon rolls and small sausages.

Honey-Roast Chicken

	Imperial	Metric	American
Chicken	*3 lb*	*1.5 kg*	*3 lb*
Salt and pepper			
Cooking apple	*1*	*1*	*1*
Large onion	*1*	*1*	*1*
Oil	*4 tbsp*	*4 tbsp*	*4 tbsp*
Clear honey	*4 tbsp*	*4 tbsp*	*4 tbsp*
Watercress			

Sprinkle the inside of the chicken with salt and pepper. Peel and core the apple, and cut it into quarters. Put them inside the chicken together with the quartered onion. Brush with a little oil and put into a roasting tin. Pour over the honey, and put the rest of the oil into the tin. Roast at 375°F/190°C/Gas Mark 5 for $1\frac{1}{4}$ hours, basting from time to time with the pan juices. Serve garnished with watercress.

Bacon-Stuffed Chicken

	Imperial	Metric	American
Roasting chicken	3 lb	1.5 kg	3 lb
Streaky bacon rashers	4 oz	100 g	4 tbsp
Small onion	1	1	1
Butter	1 oz	25 g	2 tbsp
Fresh white breadcrumbs	3 oz	75 g	1 cup
Chopped parsley	2 tbsp	2 tbsp	2 tbsp
Pepper			
Streaky bacon rashers	6	6	6

Remove the giblets from the chicken and simmer them in ½ pt/250 ml water. Cut the bacon into pieces and chop the onion. Melt the butter and cook the bacon and onion for 4 minutes until soft and golden. Stir in the breadcrumbs, parsley and pepper. Put this stuffing in the neck and body of the bird and roast at 400°F/200°C/Gas Mark 6 for 1 hour. Remove the rind from the bacon rashers and stretch the rashers with the back of a flat-bladed knife. Cut in half and roll up each piece of bacon. Thread on to skewers and cook them in the oven with the chicken for 20 minutes longer. Serve the chicken with the bacon rolls and gravy made from the giblet stock.

Spanish-Stuffed Chicken

	Imperial	Metric	American
Chicken	3 lb	1.5 kg	3 lb
Spanish stuffed green olives	3 oz	75 g	¾ cup
White bread	3 oz	75 g	3 slices
Milk	3 tbsp	3 tbsp	3 tbsp
Egg	1	1	1
Cooked ham	4 oz	100 g	½ cup
Chopped parsley	1 tbsp	1 tbsp	1 tbsp
Salt	½ tsp	½ tsp	½ tsp
Made mustard	½ tsp	½ tsp	½ tsp
Pepper			

Chop half the olives and leave the rest whole. Cut the bread in cubes, soak it in the milk, then squeeze dry. Mix together the chopped and whole olives, bread, beaten egg, finely-chopped ham, parsley and seasonings. Stuff the neck and cavity of the chicken. Roast at 350°F/180°C/Gas Mark 4 for 1¼ hours.

Slimmers' Chicken

	Imperial	Metric	American
Chicken	3 lb	1.5 kg	3 lb
Cottage cheese	5 oz	125 g	¾ cup
Chopped parsley	1 tsp	1 tsp	1 tsp
Chopped mixed herbs	1 tsp	1 tsp	1 tsp
Salt and pepper			
Butter	1 oz	25 g	2 tbsp

Combine the cottage cheese with the herbs and seasoning until they are well blended. Stuff the chicken with the herb and cheese mixture. Place a knob of butter on the chicken and then roast it at 350°F/180°C/Gas Mark 4 for 1¼ hours until golden and tender. Serve hot with a cole-slaw salad.

Prune-Stuffed Chicken

	Imperial	Metric	American
Chicken	3 lb	1.5 kg	3 lb
Prunes	4 oz	100 g	$\frac{1}{4}$ lb
White wine	3 fl.oz	75 ml	$\frac{1}{3}$ cup
Finely-minced pork	6 oz	150 g	$\frac{3}{4}$ cup
Shallot	1	1	1
Egg yolk	1	1	1
Cognac	1 tbsp	1 tbsp	1 tbsp
Salt and black pepper			
Parsley	1 tbsp	1 tbsp	1 tbsp
Pinch of thyme			

Soak the prunes in the white wine overnight.
Next day, stone them and mash to a pulp with a fork.
Stir the purée into the minced pork, together with
the finely-chopped shallot. Bind with egg yolk and
add cognac. Season well with salt, pepper, chopped
parsley and thyme. Stuff the chicken and roast at
350°F/180°C/ Gas Mark 4 for 1$\frac{1}{4}$ hours.

Sweet Corn Chicken

	Imperial	Metric	American
Chicken	3 lb	1.5 kg	3 lb
Butter	1 oz	25 g	2 tbsp
Small onion	1	1	1
Salt			
Pepper	$\frac{1}{4}$ tsp	$\frac{1}{4}$ tsp	$\frac{1}{4}$ tsp
Canned sweetcorn kernels	5 oz	125 g	small
Grated rind of lemon	$\frac{1}{2}$	$\frac{1}{2}$	$\frac{1}{2}$
Squeeze of lemon juice			
Chopped parsley	1 tbsp	1 tbsp	1 tbsp
Egg	1	1	1

Melt the butter in a saucepan, add the chopped onion and cook over gentle heat until beginning to soften. Stir in the salt, pepper and sweet corn and cook for 2 to 3 minutes. Remove from the heat, add the lemon rind and juice, the parsley and beaten egg. Mix thoroughly and fill loosely into the bird. Stuff the chicken and roast at 350°F/180°C/Gas Mark 4 for 1½ hours.

Somerset Chicken

	Imperial	Metric	American
Chicken	3 lb	1.5 kg	3 lb
Parsley and thyme stuffing	4 oz	100 g	1 cup
Soft dark brown sugar	1 tbsp	1 tbsp	1 tbsp
Lemon rind	½	½	½
Lemon juice	1 tsp	1 tsp	1 tsp
Butter	1 oz	25 g	2 tbsp
Cooking apples	8 oz	200 g	2 cups
Cider	¼ pint	125 ml	½ cup
Cornflour or cornstarch	2 tsp	2 tsp	2 tsp
Water	2 tbsp	2 tbsp	2 tbsp
Salt and pepper			

Stuff the chicken with the parsley and thyme stuffing. Mix the sugar, lemon rind and juice and butter, and spread the mixture on the breast of the chicken. Roast at 375°F/190°C/Gas Mark 5, basting frequently for 1¼ hours. Peel and core the apples and cut them into rings. Put the apple rings round the chicken and pour the cider over the bird. Continue cooking for 20 minutes. Put the chicken and apple rings on to a serving dish. Mix the cornflour and water until smooth and add to the pan juices. Stir well, season and bring to the boil. Serve each portion of chicken with some apple rings, stuffing and cider sauce.

Pineapple-Stuffed Chicken

	Imperial	Metric	American
Chicken	3 lb	1.5 kg	3 lb
Butter	2 oz	50 g	4 tbsp
Stuffing			
Onion	1 large	1 large	1 large
Butter	1 oz	25 g	2 tbsp
Stale white breadcrumbs	4 oz	100 g	2 cups
Walnuts	2 oz	50 g	$\frac{1}{2}$ cup
Seedless raisins	2 oz	50 g	$\frac{1}{2}$ cup
Grated lemon rind	$\frac{1}{2}$	$\frac{1}{2}$	$\frac{1}{2}$
Salt and pepper			
Canned pineapple slices	8 oz	200 g	medium
Extra walnut halves for garnishing			
Watercress sprigs			

Remove the giblets from the chicken and make giblet stock. To make the stuffing, soften the chopped onion in the butter without letting it brown. Stir in the breadcrumbs, chopped walnuts, raisins and lemon rind and season well. Drain 2 of the pineapple slices and chop them roughly. Add to the stuffing with 1 tbsp juice to bind and pack into the neck or body of the bird. Do not pack too tightly as the stuffing swells during cooking. Secure the neck flap in position under the wing tips and weigh the bird. Place in a roasting tin, spread with butter and cover with buttered paper. Cook at 350°F/180°C/Gas Mark 4 for $1\frac{1}{4}$ hours.

When cooked, put the bird on a serving dish. Add a little giblet stock to the tin and make gravy in the usual way. Heat the remaining pineapple slices in their juice and arrange them round the bird. Garnish with some walnut halves and watercress sprigs.

Roast Chicken with Orange and Chestnut Stuffing

	Imperial	Metric	American
Chicken	3 lb	1.5 kg	3 lb
Butter	2 oz	50 g	4 tbsp
Stuffing			
Large onion	1	1	1
Butter	1 oz	25 g	2 tbsp
Patna rice	4 oz	100 g	$\frac{3}{4}$ cup
Oranges	2	2	2
Skinned chestnuts	8 oz	200 g	2 cups
Salt and pepper			
Bay leaf	1	1	1
Egg	1	1	1

Remove the giblets from the chicken and make giblet stock. To make the stuffing, chop the onion and cook it in the butter until soft. Cook the rice in plenty of boiling salted water, drain and rinse well. Mix it with the onion. Halve each orange and cut out the flesh with a grapefruit knife. Remove all white pith and add the segments to the rice mixture. Roughly chop the chestnuts, mix all together with the seasonings and bay leaf, and bind with beaten egg. Pack into the body cavity of the bird. Secure the neck flap in position under the wing tips and weigh the bird. Spread it with butter and cover with buttered paper, placing it in a roasting tin. Cook at 350°F/180°C/Gas Mark 4 for $1\frac{1}{4}$ hours.

Fruit and Nut Chicken

	Imperial	Metric	American
Chicken	3 lb	1.5 kg	3 lb
Butter	2 oz	50 g	4 tbsp
Grated orange rind	1	1	1
Tabasco sauce	$\frac{1}{4}$ tsp	$\frac{1}{4}$ tsp	$\frac{1}{4}$ tsp
Stuffing			
Butter	1 oz	25 g	2 tbsp
Onion	1	1	1
Cooked rice	4 oz	100 g	1 cup
Liver sausage	4 oz	100 g	1 cup
Raisins	2 oz	50 g	$\frac{1}{2}$ cup
Almonds	2 oz	50 g	$\frac{1}{2}$ cup
Egg	1	1	1
Tabasco sauce	$\frac{3}{4}$ tsp	$\frac{3}{4}$ tsp	$\frac{3}{4}$ tsp
Salt and pepper			

To make the stuffing, melt the butter and fry
the chopped onion in it until soft but not brown.
Put the onion, rice, liver sausage, raisins and almonds
into a basin. Beat the egg with the Tabasco sauce,
salt and pepper. Add the egg to the stuffing, and mix
well together. Stuff the chicken in the usual way.
Cream the butter with orange rind and Tabasco
sauce. Spread the butter mixture over the chicken.
Roast at 375°F/190°C/Gas Mark 5 for $1\frac{1}{2}$ hours.

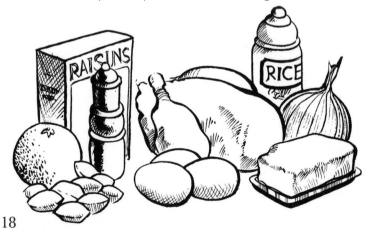

Chapter Three

GRILLED OR FRIED CHICKEN

Chicken joints can be bought at most butchers and freezer centres and provide the basis of quickly-prepared grilled and fried meals. One chicken joint serves each person generously and can be served with vegetables, rice or pasta, or salad. Grilled and fried chicken joints are also delicious cold and make an ideal buffet meal or picnic.

Cold Spicy Chicken

	Imperial	Metric	American
Chicken joints	4	4	4
Chicken stock	$\frac{1}{4}$ pint	125 ml	$\frac{1}{2}$ cup
Turmeric	1 tsp	1 tsp	1 tsp
Curry powder	1 tsp	1 tsp	1 tsp
Ground ginger	1 tsp	1 tsp	1 tsp
Mustard powder	1 tsp	1 tsp	1 tsp
Pepper	$\frac{1}{2}$ tsp	$\frac{1}{2}$ tsp	$\frac{1}{2}$ tsp
Mixed herbs	$\frac{1}{2}$ tsp	$\frac{1}{2}$ tsp	$\frac{1}{2}$ tsp
Ground mixed spice	$\frac{1}{4}$ tsp	$\frac{1}{4}$ tsp	$\frac{1}{4}$ tsp
Butter	1 oz	25 g	1 tbsp
Mango chutney			

Poach the joints in the stock until tender. Mix together the herbs and spices and sprinkle them over the drained and dried joints of chicken. Leave for 30 minutes. Brush the joints with melted butter and put under the grill until they turn golden brown and crisp. Leave to cool. Serve with mango chutney.

Country-Style Grilled Chicken

	Imperial	Metric	American
Chicken joints	4	4	4
Lemon	$\frac{1}{2}$	$\frac{1}{2}$	$\frac{1}{2}$
Butter	$1\frac{1}{2}$ oz	40 g	3 tbsp
Salt			
Rashers streaky bacon or slices bacon	2	2	2
Mushrooms	2 oz	50 g	$\frac{1}{2}$ cup
Watercress			
Potato crisps			

Rub the chicken with the cut lemon. Melt the butter in a small pan and brush it generously all over the chicken; sprinkle with salt. Lay pieces skin side down in a grill pan (rack removed) and cook under medium heat for 10–12 minutes. Turn, brush with more butter and continue grilling for a further 12–15 minutes, with one or two more applications of butter. When cooked, the skin should be crisp and golden and the juices, when the thigh is pierced with a fine skewer, should be colourless. Meanwhile, fry the bacon strips and sliced mushrooms in the remaining butter and, when cooked, add the lemon juice. Serve the chicken with this dressing poured over and garnish with watercress and potato crisps.

Best-Ever Grilled Chicken

	Imperial	Metric	American
Chicken joints	4	4	4
Lemon	1	1	1
Salt			
Melted butter	2 oz	50 g	4 tbsp
Sugar	1 oz	25 g	1 tbsp
Paprika	¼ tsp	¼ tsp	¼ tsp
Watercress			
Potato crisps			

Rub the cut lemon, squeezing it a little to release the juice, all over the chicken and sprinkle lightly with salt. Brush liberally on both sides with melted butter. Place cut side uppermost in the bottom of the grill pan (grid removed), and cook it under medium heat for 10 to 12 minutes. Turn skin side uppermost and sprinkle evenly with mixed sugar and paprika. Continue grilling for a further 10 to 15 minutes, or until cooked, brushing frequently with melted butter. This rich golden chicken needs no garnish other than a small bunch of watercress and some potato crisps.

Barbecued Chicken Grill

	Imperial	Metric	American
Chicken joints	4	4	4
Butter	2 oz	50 g	2 tbsp
Malt vinegar	4 tbsp	4 tbsp	4 tbsp
Worcestershire sauce	1 tbsp	1 tbsp	1 tbsp
Tomato purée	1 tbsp	1 tbsp	1 tbsp
Brown sugar	1 oz	25 g	1 tbsp
Finely-grated onion	1 tsp	1 tsp	1 tsp
Paprika	1 tsp	1 tsp	1 tsp
Salt	$\frac{1}{2}$ tsp	$\frac{1}{2}$ tsp	$\frac{1}{2}$ tsp
Watercress			

Melt the butter in a small saucepan and brush it liberally all over the chicken. Arrange chicken skin side down in the grill pan (rack removed), and grill it gently for 12–15 minutes. Meanwhile add the remaining ingredients to the butter in the saucepan and simmer together for two minutes. Turn the chicken, brush with barbecue sauce and continue grilling it gently, with frequent applications of sauce, for a further 12–15 minutes. To serve, pour the remaining sauce over the chicken and garnish the dish with watercress. Serve with crusty rolls and butter.

Devilled Chicken

	Imperial	Metric	American
Chicken joints	4	4	4
Plain or all-purpose flour	2 oz	50 g	2 tbsp
Salt	1½ tsp	1½ tsp	1½ tsp
Mustard powder	2 tsp	2 tsp	2 tsp
Small egg	1	1	1
Water	1 tbsp	1 tbsp	1 tbsp
Fine semolina	3 oz	75 g	3 tbsp

Oil for frying

Mix the flour, salt and mustard and put the mixture in a paper bag. Drop each chicken joint into the bag and shake it until well coated. Dip pieces in egg and water and drain well in a sieve or colander. Allow to stand for 15 to 20 minutes so the egg will get tacky. Cover well with the semolina, turning the chicken so all parts are covered. Let it stand again for a few minutes and shake off loose semolina.

Heat the fat, about 2 in/5 cm deep, till hot but not smoking. Brown the chicken pieces quickly and cover for the first half of cooking time – about 12 minutes. For a really crisp finish remove the cover for the last 10–12 minutes' cooking time. Serve hot with mashed potatoes and a green vegetable, or serve cold with potato salad, green salad and tomatoes.

Pineapple Chicken Grill

	Imperial	Metric	American
Chicken joints	4	4	4
Pineapple cubes	8 oz	200 g	medium can
Lemon juice	1 tbsp	1 tbsp	1 tbsp
Butter	2 oz	50 g	2 tbsp
Salt			
Few sprigs fresh mint			

Drain the syrup from the pineapple cubes, add the lemon juice and pour the liquid over the chicken; leave it to soak for 1 hour. Melt the butter in a small pan, drain and dry the chicken, then brush it liberally with butter on both sides and sprinkle with salt. Arrange skin side down in grill pan (rack removed) and grill gently for 10 to 12 minutes. Turn, brush with butter and continue grilling gently, with occasional applications of butter, for a further 12 to 15 minutes. Meanwhile, add the drained and dried pineapple cubes to the butter remaining in the pan; toss and heat them together for several minutes. Serve the chicken on a flat dish, arrange pineapple cubes sprinkled with finely-chopped mint between them and garnish with sprigs of mint.

Crunchy Crisp Baked Chicken

	Imperial	Metric	American
Chicken joints	4	4	4
Plain flour or all-purpose flour	1 oz	25 g	1 tbsp
Salt	1 tsp	1 tsp	1 tsp
Curry powder	½ tsp	½ tsp	½ tsp
A little evaporated milk			
Potato crisps	3 oz	75 g	¾ cup

Pre-heat oven to 350°F/180°C/Gas Mark 4. Mix the flour, salt and curry powder together. Crush the potato crisps with a rolling pin. Coat the chicken joints with the seasoned flour, then dip them in the milk and coat thickly and evenly with potato-crisp crumbs. Arrange skin side up on a baking sheet and bake for about 40 minutes. Serve hot or cold with green salad.

Chicken in the Basket

	Imperial	Metric	American
Chicken joints	4	4	4
Melted butter			
Salt and pepper			
Onions, medium	2	2	2
Bunch of watercress			

Flatten the joints as much as possible and brush them with melted butter. Season with salt and pepper. Put joints under a hot grill, turning them occasionally for about 20 minutes until cooked. Put in bowls or serving baskets and garnish with sliced raw onions and watercress. Serve with crusty bread and butter.

Surprise Chicken

	Imperial	Metric	American
Chicken legs	4	4	4
Mushrooms	4 oz	100 g	1 cup
Bunch of watercress			
Butter	1 oz	25 g	1 tbsp
Plain or all-purpose flour			
Beaten egg			
Dried breadcrumbs			
Fat for frying			
Watercress sprigs			

Put the chicken legs into salted water and boil them gently for 20 minutes. Skin the legs and remove the bones, leaving the meat on each joint intact. Chop the mushrooms and watercress finely and pack into the cavities in the chicken legs with the butter. Pull the chicken meat over the openings to seal. Dip in flour, egg and breadcrumbs twice, making sure the openings are well sealed. Fry each joint in deep fat for 10 minutes until crisp and golden and cooked through. Drain and serve garnished with some watercress sprigs.

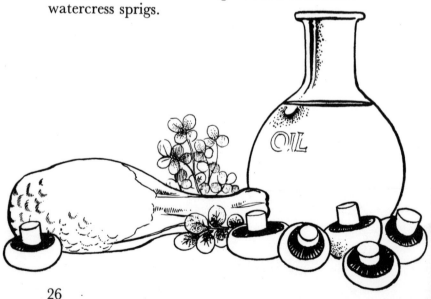

Fried Chicken with Lemon Rice

	Imperial	Metric	American
Chicken joints	4	4	4
Plain or all-purpose flour	2 oz	50 g	2 tbsp
Salt	1 tsp	1 tsp	1 tsp
Curry powder	2 tsp	2 tsp	2 tsp
Bananas	2	2	2
Long-grain rice	8 oz	200 g	2 cups
Lemon	1	1	1
Butter	2 oz	50 g	2 tbsp

Mix together the flour, salt and curry powder and coat the chicken joints with the mixture. Fry them in oil, turning once or twice, for about 10 minutes until golden. Reduce the heat, cover the pan and cook for 15 minutes until tender. Take off the lid and add the bananas (cut in halves) for 5 minutes. Meanwhile cook the rice in boiling salted water, adding a slice of lemon. Drain and remove lemon slice. Stir in butter and 2 tsp grated rind from part of the lemon. Spread the rice on a serving dish, arrange chicken and banana pieces on top, and garnish with the remaining lemon cut into slices.

Cheesey Drumsticks

	Imperial	Metric	American
Chicken drumsticks	8	8	8
Fine white breadcrumbs	4 oz	100 g	2 cups
Finely-grated cheese	2 oz	50 g	½ cup
Chopped parsley	2 tsp	2 tsp	2 tsp
Onion, small	1	1	1
Salt and pepper			
Plain or all-purpose flour	2 oz	50 g	2 tbsp
Egg	1	1	1
Deep fat for frying			

Mix together the breadcrumbs, cheese, parsley and finely-chopped onion, and season with salt and pepper. Season the flour with salt and pepper and coat the drumsticks with the seasoned flour. Dip them in beaten egg and then coat the drumsticks in the breadcrumb mixture. Repeat this coating process. Deep-fry the coated drumsticks in hot fat for 10–15 minutes until they are crisp and golden. Drain on kitchen paper. Serve hot with apple sauce, baked tomatoes and new potatoes, or cold with salad.

Chapter Four

CASSEROLES AND BAKES

Whole chickens and chicken joints are very versatile and may be cooked in a casserole or baked in a sauce. The flavour of these dishes is best if the chicken is lightly fried first in a mixture of oil and butter, which seals the flesh and keeps the chicken juicy and full of flavour. Mushrooms, onions and carrots are natural partners in a casserole, and the liquid may be chicken stock, wine or the juice from canned tomatoes. Try and use fresh herbs in these dishes, as their flavour is so much fresher.

Chicken in a Nest

	Imperial	Metric	American
Chicken joints	4	4	4
Butter	1 oz	25 g	2 tbsp
Salt and pepper			
Onion, medium	1	1	1
Mushrooms	2 oz	50 g	½ cup
Chicken stock	¼ pint	125 ml	½ cup
Canned sweetcorn	12 oz	300 g	large can

Melt the butter and in it cook the chicken portions until golden. Season with salt and pepper and put into a warm casserole. Chop the onion and slice the mushrooms and cook them in the butter until the onions are soft and golden. Add the stock and pour it over the chicken. Drain the can of corn and arrange the corn round the chicken. Cover and cook at 375°F/190°C/Gas Mark 5 for 45 minutes. Serve with a green salad.

Baked Barbecued Chicken

	Imperial	Metric	American
Chicken joints	4	4	4
Lemon juice	2 tbsp	2 tbsp	2 tbsp
Oil	3 tbsp	3 tbsp	3 tbsp
Worcestershire sauce	1 tbsp	1 tbsp	1 tbsp
Tabasco sauce	10 drops	10 drops	10 drops
Garlic clove	1	1	1
Tomato sauce	1 tbsp	1 tbsp	1 tbsp
Black pepper			
Seasoned flour			

Make deep cuts with a pointed knife into the flesh of the chicken. Mix together all the other ingredients except the flour. Pour the mixture over the chicken and leave in the refrigerator for some hours or overnight. When required, lift the joints from the marinade, roll them in seasoned flour, turn them in hot fat in an ovenware dish and bake at 375°F/190°C/Gas Mark 5 for 30 minutes, turning half-way through cooking. The remaining marinade may be stored in the refrigerator and used again.

Farmhouse Chicken-Bake

	Imperial	Metric	American
Chicken	3 lb	1.5 kg	3 lb
Seasoned flour	½ oz	15 g	½ tbsp
Rashers streaky bacon or slices bacon	4	4	4
Cider	2 tbsp	2 tbsp	2 tbsp
Fresh white breadcrumbs	8 oz	200 g	4 cups
Shredded suet or finely chopped suet	4 oz	100 g	¼ cup
onions, large	2	2	2
Rosemary	1 tsp	1 tsp	1 tsp
Grated rind of ½ lemon			
Egg	1	1	1
A little milk			

Cut the chicken into 8 pieces, toss them in seasoned flour and put in a casserole. Cover with bacon rashers and pour the cider over. Mix all the other ingredients together, chopping the onion finely and adding sufficient milk to bind. Cover the chicken with this mixture, pressing down evenly. Cover and bake at 350°F/180°C/Gas Mark 4, for 2 hours. Remove the lid and cook for a further 15 minutes to brown.

Country Chicken Dumpling Roll

	Imperial	Metric	American
Self-raising flour or flour sifted with 4 tsp baking powder	1 lb	450 g	4 cups
Salt	1 tsp	1 tsp	1 tsp
Shredded suet	6 oz	150 g	1 cup
Cooked chicken	8 oz	200 g	½ lb
Chicken livers	8 oz	200 g	½ lb
Mushrooms	8 oz	200 g	½ lb
Dried marjoram	1 tbsp	1 tbsp	1 tbsp
Salt and pepper			
Mushroom Sauce			
Butter	2 oz	50 g	2 tbsp
Mushrooms	8 oz	200 g	½ lb
Cornflour or cornstarch	2 tsp	2 tsp	2 tsp
Chicken stock	½ pint	300 ml	1¼ cups
Salt and pepper			
Tomato purée	1 tsp	1 tsp	1 tsp

To make the sauce, heat the butter and lightly fry the sliced mushrooms in it for about 4 minutes. Blend the cornflour with a little stock, add to the pan and cook for 2 minutes, stirring. Add the remaining stock. Season and bring to boil. Add tomato purée and cook for a further 2 minutes, stirring well. Pour over the Chicken Dumpling Roll or serve separately in sauce boat.

Dumpling Roll Mix flour, salt and suet with cold water to a firm pastry. Roll into a rectangle. Cover with chopped chicken, livers, mushrooms marjoram and seasoning. Roll up and put on baking sheet. Bake at 375°F/190°C/Gas Mark 5 for 45 minutes.

Chicken Mornay

	Imperial	Metric	American
Chicken	3 lb	1.5 kg	3 lb
Chicken stock	1 pint	500 ml	2½ cups
Peppercorns	6	6	6
Bay leaf	1	1	1
Sprig of rosemary			
Noodles	8 oz	200 g	2 cups
Butter	1 oz	25 g	2 tbsp
Plain or all-purpose flour	1 oz	25 g	2 tbsp
Milk	1 pint	500 ml	2½ cups
Salt and pepper			
Grated cheese	6 oz	150 g	1½ cups
Caraway seeds	2 tsp	2 tsp	2 tsp
Extra butter			

Wash the chicken and then poach it gently in the stock with the peppercorns, bay leaf and rosemary for about 1 hour or until tender. Cook the noodles in boiling salted water for 10 minutes until tender. Melt the butter, stir in the flour and cook gently for 1 minute. Blend in the milk, then thicken it over a moderate heat. Season and add the cheese. Drain the noodles and toss them in a little butter and the caraway seeds. Put on a serving dish. Place the chicken on top of the noodles and coat with the sauce. Put under the grill for a few minutes until it starts to turn golden.

33

Cheesey Chicken Crumble

	Imperial	Metric	American
Onion, small	1	1	1
Butter	1 oz	25 g	2 tbsp
Plain or all-purpose flour	1 oz	25 g	1 tbsp
Milk	$\frac{1}{4}$ pint	125 ml	$\frac{1}{2}$ cup
Chicken stock (made from a cube)	$\frac{1}{4}$ pint	125 ml	$\frac{1}{2}$ cup
Cooked chicken	6 oz	150 g	$\frac{3}{4}$–1 cup
Salt and pepper			
Worcestershire sauce	1 tsp	1 tsp	1 tsp
Tomatoes, large	2	2	2
Topping			
Plain or all-purpose flour	3 oz	75 g	3 tbsp
Pinch of salt			
Butter	$1\frac{1}{2}$ oz	40 g	3 tbsp
Cheddar cheese	2 oz	50 g	$\frac{1}{2}$ cup

Fry the finely-chopped onion in the butter until soft but not brown. Stir in the flour and cook for 1 minute. Remove from the heat and gradually stir in the milk and stock. Return it to the heat, bring to the boil, stirring, and cook for a minute. Stir in the diced chicken, seasoning and Worcestershire sauce. Put the chicken into an ovenware dish. Place slices of tomato on top of the chicken mixture. Sieve the flour and salt into a bowl and rub in the butter until the mixture resembles fine crumbs. Stir in the grated cheese. Spoon this crumble over the tomatoes. Bake at 375°F/190°C/Gas Mark 5 for 40 minutes.

Chiswick Chicken

	Imperial	Metric	American
Chicken joints	4	4	4
Butter	2 oz	50 g	4 tbsp
Tomatoes	8 oz	200 g	$\frac{1}{2}$ lb
Spring onions	4	4	4
Plain or all-purpose flour	1 oz	25 g	1 tbsp
Milk	$\frac{1}{4}$ pint	125 ml	$\frac{1}{2}$ cup
Curry powder	1 tsp	1 tsp	1 tsp
Salt and pepper			
Cooked green peas	2 oz	50 g	4 tbsp
Mushrooms	4 oz	100 g	1 cup
Commercial soured cream			
(sour cream)	5 fl.oz	125 ml	$\frac{1}{2}$ cup
Chopped parsley			

Cook the chicken joints in about $\frac{1}{2}$ pt/250 ml boiling water until tender. Skin and strip the meat from the bones and tear the meat into large pieces. Melt the butter and in it cook the peeled and chopped tomatoes and chopped spring onions until soft and golden. Stir in the flour and gradually stir in the milk and $\frac{1}{4}$ pt/125 ml of the chicken cooking liquid. Cook and stir over low heat to make a creamy sauce. Add curry powder, salt and pepper, and then stir in the peas and sliced mushrooms. Heat gently and stir in the soured cream and chicken pieces. Do not boil once the cream has been added. Serve garnished with chopped parsley.

Ginger Chicken

	Imperial	Metric	American
Chicken joints	4	4	4
Butter	4 oz	100 g	8 tbsp
Onions	2	2	2
Made mustard	2 tbsp	2 tbsp	2 tbsp
Salt and pepper			
Ground ginger	1 tsp	1 tsp	1 tsp
Orange juice	2 tbsp	2 tbsp	2 tbsp
Bottle of ginger ale	1	1	1

Melt the butter and in it brown joints all over.
Fry sliced onions in the same fat. Smear the joints
with mustard. Sprinkle with salt and pepper. Return
to the pan and add remaining ingredients. Bring to
the boil and simmer for 45 minutes.

Vineyard Chicken

	Imperial	Metric	American
Chicken joints	4	4	4
Onion	1	1	1
Mushrooms	6 oz	150 g	1½ cups
Carrots	8 oz	200 g	½ lb
Seasoned flour	½ oz	15 g	½ tbsp
White wine	¼ pint	125 ml	½ cup
Chicken stock	½ pint	250 ml	1¼ cups
Tomato sauce	1 tbsp	1 tbsp	1 tbsp
Salt and pepper			

Place the chicken, chopped onion, sliced
mushrooms and carrots in an ovenware dish. Add the
seasoned flour and mix well. Mix the wine and stock
with the tomato sauce and pour it over the chicken
and vegetables. Season and bake at 350°F/180°C/Gas
Mark 4 for 1½ hours.

Tarragon Chicken

	Imperial	Metric	American
Butter	1 oz	25 g	2 tbsp
Carrots, medium	2	2	2
Onion, medium	1	1	1
Stick of celery or stalk of celery	1	1	1
Parsley sprigs	4	4	4
Chicken	3 lb	1.5 kg	3 lb
Chicken stock	1¾ pints	1 litre	4½ cups
Tarragon	½ tsp	½ tsp	½ tsp
Clove	1	1	1
Pinch of salt			
Egg yolks	2	2	2

Melt the butter and to it add the thinly-sliced carrots, onions and celery. Cover and cook very gently for 30 minutes. Put the vegetables in a casserole with the parsley on top. Put the chicken on the vegetables and cover with boiling stock. Add the tarragon, clove and salt. Cover and cook at 325°F/ 170°C/Gas Mark 3 for 1½ hours. Drain off the chicken liquid and measure out 1 pt/500 ml. Put it into a saucepan and boil until reduced by half. Take off the heat and pour a little of the hot liquid on to the egg yolks. Work together quickly and stir in the remaining hot liquid. Pour over the chicken before serving.

Devonshire Chicken Casserole

	Imperial	Metric	American
Chicken joints	4	4	4
Butter	2 oz	50 g	4 tbsp
Onion	2 oz	50 g	4 tbsp
Stick of celery or stalk of celery	1	1	1
Rashers streaky bacon or slices bacon	2	2	2
Plain or all-purpose flour	1 oz	25 g	1 tbsp
Pepper	¼ tsp	¼ tsp	¼ tsp
Chicken stock	¾ pint	375 ml	1½ cups
Tomatoes	3	3	3

Cook the chicken joints in the butter for 10 minutes over gentle heat. Put the chicken into a casserole. Chop the onion, celery and bacon and cook them in the butter for 5 minutes. Sprinkle in the flour and pepper. Stir for a minute over heat and then stir in the stock. Peel the tomatoes, take out the seeds, and cut the flesh in quarters. Add the tomatoes to the sauce and pour it over the chicken. Cover and cook at 350°F/180°C/Gas Mark 4 for 45 minutes. Serve with mashed potatoes and peas.

Chicken in the Pot

	Imperial	Metric	American
Chicken	3 lb	1.5 kg	3 lb
Salt and pepper			
Butter	2 oz	50 g	4 tbsp
Sausage meat	4 oz	100 g	1 cup
Fresh breadcrumbs	1 tbsp	1 tbsp	1 tbsp
Chicken liver	1	1	1
Chopped parsley	1 tbsp	1 tbsp	1 tbsp
Oil	1 tbsp	1 tbsp	1 tbsp
Streaky bacon rashers or slices bacon	4 oz	100 g	6 slices
Button onions	12	12	12
Potatoes	1 lb	450 g	1 lb

Take out the giblets and season the chicken inside and out with salt and pepper. Mix together the sausage meat, breadcrumbs, chopped liver and parsley and stuff the neck of the bird with it, securing the flap of skin under the wing tips. Heat the butter and oil and in it brown the chicken all over. Add the chopped bacon and whole onions, cover closely and cook over a very gentle heat for 15 minutes. Baste the chicken, add the potatoes cut into small cubes and turn them in the fat. Put on the lid again and continue cooking in the oven at 350°F/180°C/Gas Mark 4 for 1½ hours. Serve in the casserole, sprinkling the potatoes with chopped herbs.

Country Chicken

	Imperial	Metric	American
Chicken	3 lb	1.5 kg	3 lb
Butter	1 oz	25 g	2 tbsp
Oil	2 tbsp	2 tbsp	2 tbsp
Unsmoked streaky bacon	6 oz	150 g	9 slices
Mushrooms	4 oz	100 g	1 cup
White wine	3 tbsp	3 tbsp	3 tbsp
Pinch of garlic salt			
Pepper			
Tomatoes	4	4	4
Bay leaf	1	1	1

Heat the butter and oil and in it brown the chicken all over. Put the chicken into a warm casserole. Chop the bacon and mushrooms and add them to the fat. Cook for 4 minutes, then add the wine, garlic salt and pepper, and pour the mixture over the chicken. Cover and cook at 350°F/180°C/Gas Mark 4 for 1 hour. Peel the tomatoes and cut them in slices. Add the sliced tomatoes and bay leaf to the casserole and continue cooking for 45 minutes. Remove the bay leaf before serving with baked jacket potatoes.

Stoved Chicken

	Imperial	Metric	American
Onions, large	2	2	2
Potatoes	2 lb	1 kg	2 lb
Chicken joints	4	4	4
Butter	2 oz	50 g	4 tbsp
Salt and pepper			
Chicken stock	1 pint	500 ml	2½ cups
Chopped parsley	1 tbsp	1 tbsp	1 tbsp

Cut the onions in slices and cut the potatoes in medium-thick slices. Brown the chicken joints in half the butter. Put a thick layer of potatoes in a casserole, then a layer of onions and the chicken joints. Season well with salt and pepper and dot with the remaining butter. Top with another layer of potatoes, then onions and finally potatoes. Season with salt and pepper and pour on the stock. Put on a piece of buttered greaseproof paper and a lid. Cook at 300°F/150°C/Gas Mark 2 for 2½ hours. Sprinkle with parsley before serving.

Creamed Almond Chicken

	Imperial	Metric	American
Plain or all-purpose flour	1 oz	25 g	1 tbsp
Salt and pepper			
Chicken	3 lb	1.5 kg	3 lb
Butter	1 oz	25 g	2 tbsp
Blanched almonds	1 oz	25 g	¼ cup
Stalks or sticks of celery	2	2	2
Chicken stock	¼ pint	125 ml	½ cup
Commercial soured cream			
or sour cream	2 tbsp	2 tbsp	2 tbsp

Season the flour with salt and pepper and use this to dust the chicken. Melt the butter and brown the chicken quickly on all sides. Cut the almonds in strips and cook them in the fat until golden. Put the chicken, almonds and chopped celery into a casserole with salt and pepper and chicken stock. Cover and cook at 375°F/190°C/Gas Mark 5 for 1 hour. Remove the lid and skim off excess fat. Stir the cream into the pan juices and baste the chicken. Continue cooking for 15 minutes and serve with rice.

Chicken and Mushroom Casserole

	Imperial	Metric	American
Large onion	1	1	1
Mushrooms	4 oz	100 g	1 cup
Butter	2 oz	50 g	4 tbsp
Chicken joints	4	4	4
Flour, plain/all-purpose	½ oz	15 g	½ tbsp
Salt and pepper			
Mixed herbs	1 tsp	1 tsp	1 tsp
Tomato sauce	2 tbsp	2 tbsp	2 tbsp
Chicken stock	1 pint	500 ml	2½ cups

Chop the onion, cut the mushrooms in quarters and cook them gently in the butter until the onion is soft and golden. Add the chicken joints and cook until golden on all sides. Take out the chicken joints and keep them warm. Sprinkle in the flour and seasonings and stir well. Add the herbs and the tomato sauce. Add the stock, stirring slowly until the mixture thickens. Put in the chicken joints, cover and simmer for 45 minutes, turning the chicken pieces once.

Pot Roast Chicken

	Imperial	Metric	American
Chicken	3 lb	1.5.kg	3 lb
Butter	1½ oz	40 g	3 tbsp
Sticks or stalks of celery	2	2	2
Onions, small	6	6	6
Carrots, medium	2	2	2
Turnip, small	1	1	1
Chicken stock	½ pint	250 ml	1¼ cups

Salt and pepper
Chopped parsley   1 tbsp   1 tbsp   1 tbsp

Brown the chicken lightly on all sides in the butter. Add the sliced vegetables, stock and seasoning. Cover and simmer for 2 hours, basting sometimes with the stock. Garnish with chopped parsley before serving. If preferred, the chicken may be cooked in the oven at 350°F/180°C/Gas Mark 4.

Chicken Robert

	Imperial	Metric	American
Chicken joints	4	4	4
Plain or all-purpose flour	½ oz	15 g	½ tbsp
Butter	3 oz	75 g	6 tbsp
Prunes (soaked and stoned)	8	8	8
Canned tomatoes	8 oz	200 g	2 cups
Chicken stock cube	1	1	1
White wine	½ bottle	½ bottle	½ bottle
Bay leaf	1	1	1
Parsley sprigs	3	3	3
Shelled prawns	3 oz	75 g	6 tbsp
Button mushrooms	4 oz	100 g	1 cup
Double or thick cream	1 tbsp	1 tbsp	1 tbsp

Dip the chicken in the flour. Brown it on all sides in the butter. Place in a casserole dish with the prunes and tomatoes. Tie the bay leaf and parsley stalks together with cotton and add them to the casserole with the stock cube and wine. Cover and cook at 325°F/170°C/Gas Mark 3 for 1¼ hours. Add the prawns and continue cooking for 5 minutes. Remove the bay leaf and parsley stalks. Test the seasoning. Place the chicken on a serving dish. Pour the sauce over it and garnish with whole mushrooms cooked in the butter and with a little cream dribbled over.

Covent Garden Chicken

	Imperial	Metric	American
Chicken	3 lb	1.5 kg	3 lb
Salt and pepper			
Butter	4 oz	100 g	8 tbsp
Baby carrots	12	12	12
Baby white turnips	4	4	4
Sugar	1 tsp	1 tsp	1 tsp
Baby onions	8	8	8
Small new potatoes	8	8	8
Lean bacon	4 oz	100 g	5 slices
Chicken stock	¼ pint	125 ml	½ cup
White wine	¼ pint	125 ml	½ cup

Season the chicken with salt and pepper. Melt half the butter in a strong pan and turn the chicken in the butter to brown evenly. Transfer the bird to a casserole dish. Melt the remaining butter in another pan and gently stew the carrots and turnips cut in quarters in the butter with the sugar for 2–3 minutes. Add the peeled whole onions, potatoes and chopped bacon and cook for a further 3 minutes. Turn all the vegetables into the casserole, add the stock and wine, cover and cook at 400°F/200°C/Gas Mark 6 for 30 minutes. Lift the chicken out of the casserole, joint it and return it to the dish. Serve with a green salad and French bread.

Chapter Five

INTERNATIONAL CHICKEN

Chicken is popular in every country in the world, complementing beautifully exotic spices and vegetables, blending with favourite wines and accompanying traditional rice and pasta. These days, the ingredients are obtainable everywhere, and it is fun to prepare an international chicken dish for an informal party or family meal.

Italian Chicken

	Imperial	Metric	American
Oil	4 tbsp	4 tbsp	4 tbsp
Chicken portions	4	4	4
Garlic cloves	3	3	3
Onion, large	1	1	1
Oregano	$\frac{1}{2}$ tsp	$\frac{1}{2}$ tsp	$\frac{1}{2}$ tsp
Canned tomatoes	1 lb	450 g	large
Tomato can of white wine or cider	$\frac{1}{2}$	$\frac{1}{2}$	$\frac{1}{2}$
Salt and pepper			
Macaroni	8 oz	200 g	2 cups

Heat oil and in it brown the chicken portions. Remove the chicken. Add the crushed garlic and chopped onion and fry a few seconds. Add the oregano, tomatoes, wine or cider and seasoning. Bring to the boil. Place chicken portions in a well-buttered casserole. Pour the sauce on them. Cover and cook at 350°F/180°C/Gas Mark 4 for 40–45 minutes or until chicken is tender. Cook the macaroni. Drain it well and toss in a little melted butter. Serve as an accompaniment to the chicken.

Chicken Marengo

	Imperial	Metric	American
Butter	2 oz	50 g	4 tbsp
Oil	1 tbsp	1 tbsp	1 tbsp
Chicken joints	4	4	4
Onion, small	1	1	1
Plain or all-purpose flour	$\frac{1}{2}$ oz	15 g	$\frac{1}{2}$ tbsp
Dry white wine	3 fl.oz	75 g	$\frac{1}{3}$ cup
Tomato purée	1 tbsp	1 tbsp	1 tbsp
Chicken stock	$\frac{1}{2}$ pint	250 ml	$1\frac{1}{4}$ cups
Garlic clove	1	1	1
Bay leaf	1	1	1
Salt and pepper			
Mushrooms	4 oz	100 g	1 cup

Heat the oil and butter in a heavy frying pan or iron casserole. When the butter stops foaming, put in the washed and dried joints and cook them on all sides until golden. Lift out. In the same pan, cook the chopped onion until it is soft and golden, for about 5 minutes, then sprinkle in the flour and let it brown for a minute or two. Now pour in the wine and let it bubble for a minute, then add all the remaining ingredients, except the mushrooms. Put chicken in a casserole, and pour on the sauce. Cover and cook at 375°F/190°C/Gas Mark 5 for 45 minutes or until the chicken is tender. Test by piercing the dark part of the leg with a knife – it should cut easily and show no pink. Ten minutes before serving, add the sliced mushrooms. If the sauce is too thin (it should be the consistency of pouring cream) take off the lid and allow it to reduce for 15–20 minutes.

Chicken Peking

	Imperial	Metric	American
Onion	4 oz	100 g	1 cup
Butter	2 oz	50 g	4 tbsp
Mustard powder	2 tsp	2 tsp	2 tsp
Plain or all-purpose flour	2 oz	50 g	2 tbsp
Chicken stock	$\frac{1}{2}$ pint	250 ml	$1\frac{1}{4}$ cups
Milk	$\frac{1}{4}$ pint	125 ml	$\frac{1}{2}$ cup
Parsley	2 tbsp	2 tbsp	2 tbsp
Salt	$\frac{1}{2}$ tsp	$\frac{1}{2}$ tsp	$\frac{1}{2}$ tsp
Cooked chicken	12 oz	300 g	2 cups
Noodles	8 oz	200 g	2 cups
Butter	1 oz	25 g	2 tbsp

Fry the chopped onion in the butter until
golden. Add the mustard and flour and cook for
1 minute without browning. Blend in the stock and
milk, and bring to the boil, stirring. Simmer for 3–5
minutes, then add the chopped parsley and season
to taste with salt. Add the chopped chicken and heat
through. Cook the noodles in plenty of fast-boiling
salted water for about 9 minutes, until they are just
soft but still slightly firm to bite. Drain and rinse
in cold water. Return to the pan, add the 1 oz/25 g
butter, and shake them gently over heat until piping
hot. Arrange·the noodles over the chicken, and serve
immediately.

Deep South Chicken

	Imperial	Metric	American
Onion, small	1	1	1
Mushrooms	3	3	3
Streaky bacon or bacon slices	4 oz	100 g	5 slices
Green peppers	2	2	2
Oil	4 tbsp	4 tbsp	4 tbsp
Tomatoes	4	4	4
Clear honey	6 tbsp	6 tbsp	6 tbsp
White wine	4 tbsp	4 tbsp	4 tbsp
Chicken stock	1 pint	500 ml	2½ cups
Plain or all-purpose flour	2 oz	50 g	2 tbsp
Cooked chicken	1	1	1

Lightly fry the chopped onion, mushrooms, bacon and peppers in oil. Remove them from the frying pan and arrange in a casserole with peeled chopped tomatoes. Put honey, wine and stock in the frying pan and bring to the boil. Pour the mixture into casserole. Cover and cook in a moderate oven, 350°F/180°C/Gas Mark 4, for 30 minutes. Drain the vegetables and thicken the sauce with the flour. Add the chopped chicken and vegetables to the sauce, and continue cooking for 5–10 minutes.

French Chicken

	Imperial	Metric	American
Chicken	3 lb	1.5 kg	3 lb
Salt and pepper			
Butter	2 oz	50 g	4 tbsp
Large sprig of parsley			
Chicken stock	½ pint	250 ml	1¼ cups
Onion	1	1	1

Wash and dry the bird, then sprinkle the inside with salt. Put a nut of butter and a large sprig of parsley inside the bird. Set it on a small cake rack in a roasting tin and butter it all over, just like a piece of toast, paying special attention to the drumsticks. Cover with buttered greaseproof paper. Put the sliced onion in the bottom of the roasting tin and pour round the stock. Cook at 350°F/180°C/Gas Mark 4 for 1¼ hours, basting the bird frequently with the juices in the pan. For the last half hour, remove the paper and allow the bird to brown. The juices in the bottom of the pan can be augmented with a little extra water, if they dry up. At the end you should be left with about ¼ pint/125 ml of liquid, which can be boiled for a minute or so, seasoned and served with the bird.

Portuguese Chicken

	Imperial	Metric	American
Butter	2 oz	50 g	4 tbsp
Chicken joints	4	4	4
Onion	1	1	1
Tomatoes	3	3	3
Salt and pepper			
Grated cheese	1½ oz	40 g	1½ tbsp

Melt the butter in a warm casserole. Turn the chicken joints in the butter in the casserole. Slice the onion thinly and arrange it on the chicken. Peel the tomatoes, slice them and put into the casserole. Season well and sprinkle with grated cheese. Cover and cook at 375°F/190°C/Gas Mark 5 for 40 minutes. Take off the lid and return it to the oven for 15 minutes. Serve hot with rice.

Hungarian Chicken Paprika

	Imperial	Metric	American
Chicken joints	4	4	4
Seasoned flour	1½ oz	40 g	1½ tbsp
Onions	8 oz	200 g	2 cups
Butter	2 oz	50 g	4 tbsp
Paprika	1 tbsp	1 tbsp	1 tbsp
Tomato juice	¼ pint	125 ml	½ cup
Sugar	1 tsp	1 tsp	1 tsp
Salt	1 tsp	1 tsp	1 tsp
Bay leaf	1	1	1
Yogurt or commercial soured cream	¼ pint	125 ml	½ cup

Skin the chicken joints and coat them thoroughly all over with seasoned flour. Fry the chopped onions in butter very gently till soft but not brown. Move them to one side of the pan. Add the chicken and fry till golden for 5–7 minutes. Combine the paprika, tomato juice, sugar and salt and pour them over the chicken. Add the bay leaf. Cover the pan and simmer for 45–60 minutes. Transfer the chicken to a warm dish, stir yogurt or sour cream into the sauce and reheat, without boiling, for 2–3 minutes. Pour over the chicken. Serve with potatoes, rice or dumplings.

Parisian Chicken

	Imperial	Metric	American
Chicken	3 lb	1.5 kg	3 lb
Back bacon	4 oz	100 g	5 slices
Chicken livers	4 oz	100 g	1 cup
Onion, small	1	1	1
Butter	3 oz	75 g	6 tbsp
Brandy	2 tbsp	2 tbsp	2 tbsp
Garlic clove	1	1	1
Fresh breadcrumbs	2 oz	50 g	1 cup
Grated lemon rind	1	1	1
Salt and pepper			
Egg	1	1	1

Bone the chicken or ask the butcher to do it for you. Chop the bacon, livers and onion finely and fry them in half the butter until soft and golden but not brown. Pour in the brandy. Crush the garlic and add it to the mixture with the breadcrumbs, lemon rind and seasoning, and bind it with the egg. Push the stuffing into the boned chicken, secure the opening and mould the bird into shape. Grease a piece of foil with the remaining butter and wrap the chicken in it. Simmer it in boiling water for 1 hour and then let it cool in the water. Carve downwards to serve so everyone gets a portion of chicken and stuffing. Serve with salad and new potatoes.

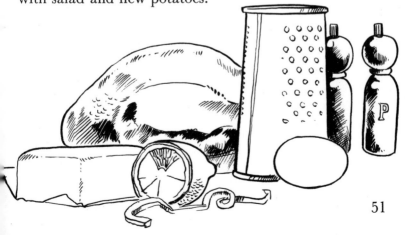

Chicken Cacciatore

	Imperial	Metric	American
Chicken joints	4	4	4
Salt and pepper			
Oil	2 tbsp	2 tbsp	2 tbsp
Onion, small	1	1	1
Garlic clove	1	1	1
Tomatoes	3	3	3
Mushrooms	2 oz	50 g	½ cup
Chicken stock	3 tbsp	3 tbsp	3 tbsp
Tomato purée	1 tbsp	1 tbsp	1 tbsp
Sherry	1 tbsp	1 tbsp	1 tbsp

Season the chicken joints and cook the chicken in the oil until golden. Add the chopped onion and crushed garlic and cook until the onion is soft and golden. Drain off any excess oil. Peel and chop the tomatoes and slice the mushrooms. Add them to the pan and stir in the stock, tomato purée and sherry. Cover and simmer for 45 minutes.

American Chicken

	Imperial	Metric	American
White sauce	½ pint	250 ml	1 cup
Single or thin cream	¼ pint	125 ml	½ cup
Mushrooms	4 oz	100 g	1 cup
Green pepper	1	1	1
Butter	2 oz	50 g	4 tbsp
Canned red pepper	1	1	1
Cooked chicken	12 oz	300 g	2 cups
Salt and pepper			
Egg yolk	1	1	1
Dry sherry	2 tbsp	2 tbsp	2 tbsp

If possible, make the white sauce with half milk and half chicken stock. Stir in the cream and heat gently. Slice the mushrooms, chop the pepper finely, and cook them in the butter for 10 minutes over low heat. Add them to the cream sauce with the red pepper cut in strips and the diced chicken. Season with salt and pepper and simmer for 5 minutes. Remove from the heat and stir in the egg yolk and sherry. Heat very gently without boiling. Serve with rice or as a vol-au-vent filling.

Chicken Nicoise

	Imperial	Metric	American
Olive oil	3 tbsp	3 tbsp	3 tbsp
Onion, small	1	1	1
Mushrooms	4 oz	100 g	1 cup
Parsley	2 tbsp	2 tbsp	2 tbsp
Salt and pepper			
Chicken stock	1 pint	500 ml	2½ cups
Canned tomatoes	8 oz	200 g	2 cups
Macaroni	12 oz	300 g	2 cups
Butter	2 oz	50 g	4 tbsp
Cooked chicken	1 lb	450 g	1 lb

Heat the oil in a pan. Add the chopped onion and sliced mushrooms and cook gently for 10 minutes. Add the parsley, salt, pepper, stock and sieved tomatoes. Stir well, bring to the boil, then simmer until the mixture has thickened and reduced in volume. Cook the macaroni as directed on the packet. Drain well, and then toss it in the melted butter. Cut the chicken into small pieces, add it to the sauce and bring to the boiling point. Pile the macaroni on to a serving dish, make a well in the centre and pour in the chicken mixture.

Maryland Kebabs with Mushroom Sauce

	Imperial	Metric	American
Marinade			
Soft brown sugar	1 oz	25 g	2 tbsp
Worcestershire sauce	1 tbsp	1 tbsp	1 tbsp
Lemon juice	2 tbsp	2 tbsp	2 tbsp
Salt			
Kebabs			
Chicken breasts	2	2	2
Baby onions	8	8	8
Streaky bacon rashers or slices	6	6	6
Bananas	3	3	3
Red pepper, large	1	1	1
Sauce			
Butter	1 oz	25 g	2 tbsp
Onion, small	1	1	1
Flat mushrooms	6 oz	150 g	$1\frac{1}{2}$ cups
Plain or all-purpose flour	$\frac{1}{2}$ oz	15 g	$\frac{1}{2}$ tbsp
Beef stock	$\frac{1}{2}$ pint	250 ml	$1\frac{1}{4}$ cups
Single or thin cream	4 tbsp	4 tbsp	4 tbsp
Worcestershire sauce	1 tbsp	1 tbsp	1 tbsp
Salt and pepper			

Blend together the marinade ingredients. Cut the chicken into 2-in/5-cm pieces. Marinate them for 4 hours in a cool place or 2 hours in a refrigerator. Place the onions in a pan of boiling water and simmer for 10 minutes. Stretch the bacon on a board with a round-bladed knife and cut each rasher in half. Drain the chicken and reserve the marinade. Cut each banana into 4, wrap each piece in a bit of bacon and dip in the marinade.

Assemble the chicken, bacon-wrapped bananas,

onions and red pepper cut in 1-in/2.5-cm pieces alternately on 4 skewers. Brush with marinade and place under a moderately hot grill for 7 minutes, then turn them and grill for a further 7 minutes, basting once with marinade. Serve the kebabs on a bed of boiled rice.

For the sauce, melt the butter in a pan and fry the chopped onion in it gently for 5 minutes. Add the chopped mushrooms and cook for 2 minutes. Stir in the flour and cook for 1 minute. Remove from the heat and blend in the stock. Return to the heat and bring it to the boil, stirring. Simmer for 3 minutes and stir in the cream and Worcestershire sauce. Season and serve hot with the kebabs.

German Chicken

	Imperial	Metric	American
Chicken breasts	4	4	4
Butter	1 oz	25 g	2 tbsp
Oil	2 tbsp	2 tbsp	2 tbsp
Mushrooms	2 oz	50 g	$\frac{1}{2}$ cup
White wine	4 tbsp	4 tbsp	4 tbsp
Walnut halves	2 oz	50 g	$\frac{1}{2}$ cup

Wipe the chicken breasts. Heat the butter and oil in a pan and in it brown the chicken pieces on all sides. Add the sliced mushrooms, wine and walnuts. Cover the pan, reduce the heat and simmer for 15–20 minutes. Remove the chicken breasts, mushrooms and walnuts to a heated serving dish. Bring the pan juices to the boil and boil steadily for several minutes to reduce and thicken. Spoon the juices over the chicken and serve with new potatoes and a green salad.

Chicken Pilaff

	Imperial	Metric	American
Chicken joints	4	4	4
Butter	2 oz	50 g	4 tbsp
Red wine or cider	$\frac{1}{4}$ pint	125 ml	$\frac{1}{2}$ cup
Redcurrant jelly	1 tbsp	1 tbsp	1 tbsp
Almonds or cashew nuts	1 oz	25 g	$\frac{1}{4}$ cup
Pilaff			
Onion, medium	1	1	1
Butter	$1\frac{1}{2}$ oz	40 g	3 tbsp
Long-grain rice	8 oz	200 g	2 cups
Chicken stock	$1\frac{1}{4}$ pints	625 ml	3 cups
Salt and pepper			
Dried apple rings	3	3	3
Dried apricots	2 oz	50 g	6 tbsp
Dried apples	2 oz	50 g	6 tbsp
Currants	2 oz	50 g	6 tbsp

Soak the apple rings and apricots overnight.
Set the oven at 350°F/180°C/Gas Mark 4. Spread the
chicken portions with butter and put them in a roasting
tin. Pour half the wine or cider over them. Roast
them for 35 minutes, raising the heat to 400°F/200°C/
Gas Mark 6 for the last 5 minutes to brown them
thoroughly. Meanwhile, prepare the pilaff. Using a
flameproof casserole, cook the onion in 1 oz/25 g
butter until just coloured. Add the rice and stir well.
Add 1 pt/500 ml stock, season and bring to the boil.
Cover and put the casserole in the oven under the
chicken dish for 12 minutes, or until barely cooked.
While rice is cooking, stew the apricots and apples
for 10 minutes in the water in which they have been
soaked. Drain them and cut into pieces. Add the
currants. Stir the fruit carefully into the rice with a
fork. If necessary, moisten with a little stock. Season

well and dot with the remaining butter. Cover with foil and a lid and replace in oven on lower shelf. Leave for 15–20 minutes, forking the rice over once or twice. When the rice is dry, remove it from the oven. Remove the chicken and make up the gravy in the pan using the remaining wine or cider and some of the stock. Add the red-currant jelly and boil together well. Fry the nuts in a little butter until brown. Serve the chicken portions on the rice. Spoon a little gravy over each piece, serving the remainder in a sauceboat. Scatter the nuts over the chicken and serve hot.

Chicken Pompadour

	Imperial	Metric	American
Spaghetti	8 oz	200 g	2 cups
Salt and pepper			
Butter	2 oz	50 g	4 tbsp
Cooked chicken	12 oz	300 g	2 cups
Single or thin cream	$\frac{1}{4}$ pint	125 ml	$\frac{1}{2}$ cup
Egg yolk	1	1	1
Chopped parsley	1 tsp	1 tsp	1 tsp
Hot tomato sauce	$\frac{1}{2}$ pint	250 ml	$1\frac{1}{4}$ cups

Boil the spaghetti in boiling salted water until tender, but do not break it in pieces. Drain it in a colander. Grease a basin with half the butter and line it with the spaghetti, twisting it round to fit the basin. Chop the chicken, season it and mix with cream, egg yolk and parsley. Put into the spaghetti-lined basin and top with spaghetti. Cover with foil and steam for 1 hour. Turn out on to a hot dish and serve with tomato sauce. Canned tomato soup may be used for the sauce.

Poona Chicken

	Imperial	Metric	American
Chicken joints	4	4	4
Chicken stock	1 pint	500 ml	2½ cups
White wine	2 tbsp	2 tbsp	2 tbsp
Salt and pepper			
Curry sauce			
Onion, small	1	1	1
Butter	½ oz	15 g	½ tbsp
Oil	1 tbsp	1 tbsp	1 tbsp
Curry powder	2 tbsp	2 tbsp	2 tbsp
Curry paste	1 tsp	1 tsp	1 tsp
White wine	¼ pint	125 ml	½ cup
Lemon juice			
Salt			
Sugar			
Mayonnaise			
Apricot or apple purée	3 tbsp	3 tbsp	3 tbsp
Yogurt	¼ pint	125 ml	½ cup
Cold cooked rice	1 lb	450 g	3 cups
Canned pineapple cubes	8 oz	200 g	2 cups
Canned red pepper	5 oz	125 g	1 cups
Paprika			
Split toasted almonds	2 oz	50 g	½ cup

Poach the chicken in the stock and wine for 30 minutes. Remove the meat from the bones and let it cool. To prepare the sauce, fry the chopped onion gently in butter and oil until transparent. Add the curry powder and paste and cook for 2–3 minutes. Stir in the wine, stock and lemon juice, adding sugar and salt to taste. Cook without a lid over medium heat for 15 minutes so that the liquid reduces a little. Sieve and leave to cool. Beat into the mayonnaise, adding apricot or apple purée to give a good coating consistency. Finally beat in the yogurt. Adjust the seasoning, then pour the sauce over the chicken and toss it well. Chill slightly. Meanwhile mix the cold rice with cubes of pineapple and strips of red pepper. Arrange round the edge of a serving dish and pile the chicken in the centre. Dust with paprika and toss the toasted almonds over the chicken before serving.

Alabama Chicken

	Imperial	Metric	American
Plain or all-purpose flour	1 oz	25 g	1 tbsp
Salt	1 tsp	1 tsp	1 tsp
Curry powder	1 tsp	1 tsp	1 tsp
Chicken joints	4	4	4
Oil for frying			
Bananas	2	2	2
Streaky bacon rashers or slices	4	4	4
Canned sweetcorn	12 oz	300 g	3 cups
Watercress			

Mix together the flour, salt and curry powder and coat the chicken joints with the mixture. Cook the joints in oil for 10 minutes, turning once or twice until golden. Cover and continue cooking for 15 minutes. Peel the bananas, cut them in half lengthwise and then across to make each banana into four pieces. Take off the lid and add the banana pieces and bacon rashers to the fat. Cook for 5 minutes. Heat the corn and drain off the liquid. Arrange the corn on a serving dish and put the chicken pieces on top. Surround it with the banana pieces and bacon and garnish with watercress.

Neapolitan Chicken

	Imperial	Metric	American
Chicken joints	4	4	4
Seasoned flour			
Olive oil	3 tbsp	3 tbsp	3 tbsp
Lemon juice	2 tbsp	2 tbsp	2 tbsp
Salt and pepper			
Grated Parmesan cheese	2 oz	50 g	2 tbsp
Breadcrumbs	1 oz	25 g	½ cup
Oil for frying			
Spaghetti	6 oz	150 g	1½ cups
Butter	½ oz	15 g	1 tbsp

Coat the chicken joints lightly with seasoned
flour. Mix together the olive oil, lemon juice, salt and
pepper, pour this over the chicken and leave it for
1 hour. Mix three-quarters of the cheese with the
breadcrumbs and coat the chicken joints with it. Fry
the chicken in hot oil for 25 minutes, turning it as
necessary. Meanwhile, cook the spaghetti in boiling
salted water for 15 minutes until tender. Drain and
toss it in butter and remaining cheese. Put the
spaghetti on to a serving dish and arrange the chicken
pieces on top. Serve with a green salad.

Chapter Six

SAUCY CHICKEN

The delicate flavour of chicken blends well
with richly-flavoured sauces. Fruit sauces as well as
barbecue, curry, cream, wine and mushroom ones are
all good, either with freshly-cooked chicken joints or
to extend cooked chicken. Boiled rice, mashed potatoes
or new potatoes are ideal accompaniments to contrast
with these sauces, or the dishes may be served with
crusty French bread and a green salad.

Chicken in Sherry Sauce

	Imperial	*Metric*	*American*
Chicken joints	4	4	4
Salt and pepper			
Butter	2 oz	50 g	4 tbsp
Green peppers	2	2	2
Dry sherry	6 tbsp	6 tbsp	6 tbsp
Chopped parsley	1 tbsp	1 tbsp	1 tbsp
Lemon	1	1	1

Season the chicken joints and cook them in the
butter on low heat for 5 minutes on each side. Cut
the peppers into neat strips and add them to the pan.
Cook for 15 minutes, turning them frequently until
the chicken is tender. Put the chicken on a serving
dish and keep it warm. Pour the sherry into the pan
juices, stir well and pour it over the chicken.
Sprinkle with parsley and garnish with lemon quarters.
Serve with new potatoes and a green salad.

Golden Fruited Chicken

	Imperial	Metric	American
Chicken joints	4	4	4
Rosé wine	$\frac{1}{4}$ pint	125 ml	$\frac{1}{2}$ cup
Honey	2 tbsp	2 tbsp	2 tbsp
Butter	2 oz	50 g	4 tbsp
Dried apricots	4 oz	100 g	1 cup

Wipe the chicken joints and put them into a dish with the wine. Leave in a cold place for 2 hours. Remove the chicken from the wine and dry it thoroughly. Mix the honey and butter together and spread generously on the chicken pieces, reserving about one-quarter of the mixture. Put the apricots into a bowl, pour some boiling water over and leave them to stand for 10 minutes. Put the wine in the bottom of a casserole and add the drained apricots and the chicken joints. Cover and cook at 350°F/180°C/Gas Mark 4 for 45 minutes. Take out the chicken pieces and put them cut side down on a grilling rack. Brush them with the reserved honey mixture and grill until golden. Serve with the apricot and wine sauce, and with new potatoes and peas or beans.

Saucy Chicken

	Imperial	Metric	American
Chicken joints	4	4	4
Butter	1 oz	25 g	2 tbsp
Made mustard	2 tsp	2 tsp	2 tsp
Tomato chutney	2 tsp	2 tsp	2 tsp
Cayenne pepper	$\frac{1}{4}$ tsp	$\frac{1}{4}$ tsp	$\frac{1}{4}$ tsp

Brush the joints with melted butter and cook them under a hot grill for 3–4 minutes each side, then reduce the heat and grill them for about 7 minutes each side, or until cooked through. Meanwhile, mix the mustard, chutney and cayenne pepper together. As soon as the chicken is ready, spread half the mixture over each joint, put them back under a medium-hot grill and cook for 2 minutes. Serve with sauté potatoes and a salad. Heat remaining mustard mixture and serve as sauce.

Chicken in Yogurt Sauce

	Imperial	Metric	American
Butter	$\frac{1}{2}$ oz	15 g	1 tbsp
Onion, large	1	1	1
Chicken joints	4	4	4
Green pepper, large	1	1	1
Salt and pepper			
Natural yogurt	$\frac{1}{2}$ pint	250 ml	$1\frac{1}{4}$ cups
Plain or all-purpose flour	$\frac{1}{2}$ oz	15 g	$\frac{1}{2}$ tbsp

Grease an ovenware dish with the butter. Slice the onion into rings and put them on the base of the dish. Put the chicken joints on top. Cut the stem from the pepper, remove the seeds and cut the flesh into rings. Arrange the rings on the chicken and season well with salt and pepper. Pour the yogurt on it, cover with foil or a lid and cook at 375°F/190°C/Gas Mark 5 for 1 hour. Blend the flour with a little water until smooth. Add a little hot liquid from the chicken and mix well, then return it to the dish. Do not cover again, but continue cooking for 20 minutes. Serve with rice and a green salad.

Chicken and Fruit Curry

	Imperial	Metric	American
Desiccated coconut or flaked coconut	1 oz	25 g	1 tbsp
Boiling water	$\frac{1}{4}$ pint	125 ml	$\frac{1}{2}$ cup
Small onions	2	2	2
Butter	2 oz	50 g	4 tbsp
Plain or all-purpose flour	1 oz	25 g	1 tbsp
Curry powder	2 tsp	2 tsp	2 tsp
Curry paste (or concentrated curry sauce)	1 tsp	1 tsp	1 tsp
Chicken stock	1 pint	500 ml	$2\frac{1}{2}$ cups
Cooking apple	1	1	1
Pear	1	1	1
Banana	1	1	1
Dried apricots	2 oz	50 g	$\frac{1}{2}$ cup
Sultanas	2 oz	50 g	$\frac{1}{2}$ cup
Cooked chicken	12 oz	300 g	2 cups
Double or thick cream	3 fl.oz	75 ml	$\frac{1}{2}$ cup
Lemon juice	2 tbsp	2 tbsp	2 tbsp
Salt			

Soak the coconut in boiling water and leave it aside. Chop the onions finely and cook them in the butter until soft and golden. Take them off the heat and stir in the flour, curry powder and paste or concentrated sauce. Replace over heat and cook gently for 5 minutes. Strain off the coconut liquid and mix it with the chicken stock (which may be made from a stock cube). Add this to the pan and simmer for 30 minutes. Peel and core the apple and pear and cut them into neat pieces. Slice the banana. Put the chopped apricots and sultanas in hot water to soak for 5 minutes, then drain them. Add all the fruit to the curry sauce and stir in the chicken, chopped in

neat pieces. Heat through and just before serving stir
in the cream and lemon juice, and season with salt.
Serve with boiled rice and poppadums. This curry
may also be served chilled with cold rice salad and
other salads.

Slimmers' Orange Chicken

	Imperial	Metric	American
Butter	½ oz	15 g	½ tbsp
Onion, small	1	1	1
Orange, large	1	1	1
Worcestershire sauce	2 tbsp	2 tbsp	2 tbsp
Tomato purée	1 tsp	1 tsp	1 tsp
Salt and pepper			
Chicken joints	4	4	4
Sprigs of watercress			

Melt the butter and in it cook the finely-chopped
onion for 5 minutes until soft and golden. Pare thin
strips of peel from half the orange with a potato
peeler, and cut it into 'match-sticks'. Grate the
remaining orange rind and squeeze out the orange
juice. Add the orange match-sticks, grated rind and
juice to the onion with the Worcestershire sauce and
tomato purée. Bring to the boil and season to taste.
Put chicken joints on to a large piece of foil in a
roasting tin, and spoon the orange sauce over. Cover
completely in foil and bake at 400°F/200°C/Gas Mark 6
for 30 minutes. Uncover and bake for 15 minutes until
golden brown. Spoon the roasting juices over the
chicken to serve, and garnish with watercress. The
chicken pieces are also delicious to eat cold with salad.

Chicken in Mushroom Sauce

	Imperial	Metric	American
Chicken joints	4	4	4
Oil	1 tbsp	1 tbsp	1 tbsp
Butter	1 oz	25 g	2 tbsp
Onion, small	1	1	1
Condensed mushroom soup	1 tin	1 tin	1 can
Milk	¼ pint	125 ml	½ cup
Single or thin cream	3 tbsp	3 tbsp	3 tbsp
Lemon juice	1 tsp	1 tsp	1 tsp

Cook the chicken joints in the oil and butter until golden, turning them from time to time. Chop onion and cook in fat until soft. Mix the soup and milk together and pour over the chicken. Cover and simmer for 30 minutes, stirring occasionally. Take off the lid, stir in the cream and lemon juice and serve at once.

Chicken with Curry Sauce

	Imperial	Metric	American
Chicken joints	4	4	4
Salt and pepper			
Butter	1 oz	25 g	2 tbsp
Oil	2 tbsp	30 ml	2 tbsp
Sauce			
Butter	1 oz	25 g	2 tbsp
Plain flour	1 oz	25 g	2 tbsp
Curry powder	2 tsp	2 tsp	2 tsp
Salt and pepper			
Pinch of garlic salt			
Stock	½ pint	25 ml	1¼ cups
Single or thin cream	7 fl.oz	175 ml	1 cup

Season the chicken and fry in butter and oil very gently for 15 minutes each side. To make the sauce, melt the butter and stir in the flour and curry powder. Mix in the salt and pepper, garlic salt and stock and simmer for 5 minutes. Take off the heat, stir in the cream and serve with fried chicken.

Chicken in Lemon Sauce

	Imperial	Metric	American
Chicken joints	4	4	4
Seasoned flour	2 oz	50 g	4 tbsp
Butter	2 oz	50 g	4 tbsp
Olive oil	2 tbsp	2 tbsp	2 tbsp
White wine	$\frac{1}{2}$ pint	250 ml	$1\frac{1}{4}$ cups
Chicken stock	$\frac{1}{2}$ pint	250 ml	$1\frac{1}{4}$ cups
Lemon	1	1	1
A little saffron powder			
Single or thin cream	2 tbsp	2 tbsp	2 tbsp
Salt and pepper			
Black and green olives			

Toss the chicken joints in seasoned flour and fry them slowly in the butter and oil until golden brown. Stir in the remaining flour and cook for 1 minute. Add the wine and chicken stock, and the lemon cut into slices. Transfer to a flameproof casserole. Cover and cook for 40 minutes until the chicken is tender. Lift on to a warm serving dish. Stir the saffron into the liquid. Cool it slightly and add the cream. Adjust the seasoning. Pour the sauce over the chicken and garnish with black and green olives. Dust with paprika. Serve with new potatoes.

Chicken and Barbecue Sauce

	Imperial	Metric	American
Chicken joints	4	4	4
Salt and pepper			
Oil	2 tbsp	2 tbsp	2 tbsp
Butter	1 oz	25 g	2 tbsp
Onion, large	1	1	1
Tomato purée	2 tsp	2 tsp	2 tsp
Plain or all-purpose flour	2 tsp	2 tsp	2 tsp
Mustard powder	2 tsp	2 tsp	2 tsp
Soft brown sugar	1 oz	25 g	1 tbsp
Water	$\frac{1}{4}$ pint	125 ml	$\frac{1}{2}$ cup
Vinegar	2 tbsp	2 tbsp	2 tbsp
Worcestershire sauce	2 tbsp	2 tbsp	2 tbsp

Season the chicken joints and brush them with oil. Remove the grid from the grill pan and grill the chicken, turning as necessary, for about 12 minutes each side. Melt the butter and cook the chopped onion until soft. Stir in the tomato purée and cook for 2 minutes. Mix the flour, mustard, sugar, water, vinegar and Worcestershire sauce to a smooth cream and stir it into the onion mixture. Simmer for 10 minutes and serve with the grilled chicken.

Grapefruit Chicken

	Imperial	Metric	American
Chicken joints	4	4	4
Seasoned flour			
Butter	2 oz	50 g	4 tbsp
Oil	2 tbsp	2 tbsp	2 tbsp
Brandy	1 tbsp	1 tbsp	1 tbsp
Chicken stock	¼ pint	125 ml	½ cup
Sherry	4 tbsp	4 tbsp	4 tbsp
Salt and pepper			
Grapefruit	1	1	1

Dust the chicken with the flour and brown the chicken joints in the butter and oil until golden. Reduce the heat and cook the chicken gently until tender. Drain off the fat. Pour on the brandy and touch it with a lighted match. Let the flames subside and put the chicken on to a serving dish, keeping it hot. Add the chicken stock, sherry and seasoning to the pan. Cut the grapefruit in half and squeeze in the juice of one half. Stir well and cook it down to half the original quantity of liquid. Remove the sections from the second half of the grapefruit and skin them. Stir the sections into the sauce and pour over the chicken joints.

Dairy Chicken

	Imperial	Metric	American
Chicken joints	4	4	4
Salt and pepper			
Milk	1 pint	500 ml	2½ cups
Onion, small	1	1	1
Cloves	2	2	2
Plain or all-purpose flour	2 tsp	2 tsp	2 tsp
Egg	1	1	1
Bananas, small	2	2	2

Cover the chicken joints with warm water in a saucepan, season with salt, bring to the boil, remove any scum, replace lid and cook gently for 15 minutes. Drain off the liquid (use for soup), pour in the milk and add the onion stuck well with cloves. Simmer gently for 30 minutes. Remove the chicken pieces and keep them hot. Thicken the milk with the flour, then stir in the beaten egg. Cook and stir over a gentle heat until very smooth and creamy, and season to taste with pepper and salt. Pour a little of the sauce over the joints. Garnish with very thinly-sliced bananas and serve the remaining sauce separately. Serve with green peas as a colour contrast.

Honey Curry Chicken

	Imperial	Metric	American
Chicken	3 lb	1.5 kg	3 lb
Lemon	½	½	½
Clear honey	8 oz	200 g	12 tbsp
Tomato chutney	6 oz	150 g	6 tbsp
Curry powder	1 tbsp	1 tbsp	1 tbsp
Long-grain rice	4 oz	100 g	¼ lb
Mayonnaise	2 tbsp	2 tbsp	2 tbsp
Double or thick cream	¼ pint	125 ml	½ cup
Lemon juice	2 tsp	2 tsp	2 tsp

Roast the chicken with the lemon inside at 350°F/180°C/Gas Mark 4 for 1¼ hours. Allow to cool, then joint it. Melt the honey, chutney and curry powder in a pan. Bring to the boil, simmer over low heat for 10 minutes and cool. Cook the rice, rinse it with cold water and leave in a colander to drain. Line the dish with rice and arrange the chicken joints on top. Fold the mayonnaise, cream and lemon juice into the honey-curry sauce and spoon it over the chicken. Serve with banana slices, desiccated coconut and poppadums as side dishes.

Curried Chicken with Rice

	Imperial	Metric	American
Chicken joints	4	4	4
Oil	2 tbsp	2 tbsp	2 tbsp
Butter	1 oz	25 g	2 tbsp
Onions	8 oz	200 g	2 cups
Plain or all-purpose flour	½ oz	15 g	½ tbsp
Curry powder	1 oz	25 g	1 tbsp
Chicken stock	1 pint	500 ml	2½ cups
Eating apple	1	1	1
Sultanas	4 oz	100 g	1 cup
Salt and pepper			
Long-grain rice	8 oz	200 g	2 cups

Fry the chicken in oil and butter until golden. Remove it from the fat and keep it warm. Chop the onions and fry them in the fat until golden and soft. Stir in the flour and curry powder and fry for 2 minutes. Add the stock, chopped apple, sultanas and seasoning, and stir well. Add the chicken joints, bring to the boil and simmer gently for 45 minutes. Cook the rice in boiling salted water for 12 minutes, drain well and serve with the chicken plus mango chutney or other side dishes.

Chapter Seven

CHICKEN PIES

Use short-crust or puff pastry to make delicious chicken pies, in deep dishes, individual patty tins or sandwich tins. Pastry is a clever extra ingredient to extend leftover cold chicken made succulent with creamy sauce, bacon or mushrooms, plenty of herbs and seasoning.

Chicken Plate Pie

	Imperial	Metric	American
Eggs	2	2	2
Milk	$\frac{1}{4}$ *pint*	*125 ml*	$\frac{1}{2}$ *cup*
Tarragon	*1 tsp*	*1 tsp*	*1 tsp*
Grated rind $\frac{1}{2}$ lemon			
Salt and pepper			
Cooked chicken	*1 lb*	*450 g*	*3 cups*
Shortcrust pastry	*12 oz*	*300 g*	$\frac{3}{4}$ *lb*

Beat together the eggs and milk until well blended. Add the tarragon, lemon rind, salt and pepper, and the chicken cut into dice. Reserve one-third of the pastry and roll out the remainder to a 9-in/22.5-cm circle. Use it to line a 7-in/17.7-cm sandwich tin, leaving a small overlap. Fill it with the chicken and dampen the edges of the pastry. Roll out the remaining pastry into an 8-in/20-cm circle and cover the pie. Seal the edges and flute them. Make six 1-in/2.5-cm slits from the centre of the pie and fold them back to make a star. Bake at 425°F/220°C/Gas Mark 7 for 20 minutes. Reduce heat to 350°F/180°C/Gas Mark 4 and bake for 30 minutes. Serve hot or cold.

Summer Chicken Pie

	Imperial	Metric	American
Chicken	3 lb	1.5 kg	3 lb
Water	½ pint	250 ml	1¼ cups
Worcestershire sauce	2 tbsp	2 tbsp	2 tbsp
Bay leaves	2	2	2
Peppercorns	6	6	6
Sprig of parsley			
Sprig of thyme			
Onion	1	1	1
Cloves	6	6	6
Carrot	1	1	1
Plain or all-purpose flour	10 oz	250 g	10 tbsp
Mixed lard and butter	5 oz	125 g	10 tbsp
Pinch of salt			
Cold water	3 tbsp	3 tbsp	3 tbsp
Cooked bacon or ham	6 oz	150 g	¾ cup
Milk or beaten egg for glazing			

Put the chicken into a large pan with the water, Worcestershire sauce, bay leaves, peppercorns, parsley, thyme, onion spiked with cloves, and carrot. Cover it tightly, bring to the boil and simmer gently for 50 minutes until tender. Save the stock. Leave the chicken to cool, then remove the meat and chop it coarsely. Make the pastry by sifting the flour and salt together, then rubbing in the fats until the mixture is like fine breadcrumbs. Add water and mix to a firm dough. Turn on to a floured surface and knead it lightly until smooth. Roll out into a circle 12 in/30 cm in diameter. Cut out one quarter. Use the larger piece of pastry to line a 7-in/17.5-cm sandwich tin, joining the seam. Place half the chopped chicken in the base of the pie, add the chopped bacon or ham and cover it with the remaining chicken. Spoon over 3 tbsp of the chicken stock. Roll out the remaining pastry to a 7-in/17.5-cm circle to make a lid. Cover the pie, trim and seal the edges, and leave a small hole in the centre of the lid. Brush the crust with milk or beaten egg. Bake at 400°F/200°C/Gas Mark 6 for 30 minutes, then reduce the temperature to 350°F/180°C/Gas Mark 4 for 30 minutes. If the top of the pie browns too quickly, cover it with foil. Leave the pie in the tin to cool. When the pie is nearly cold, pour a little stock through the hole in the centre of the lid and leave it in a cold place until set.

Chicken Lattice Pie

	Imperial	Metric	American
White sauce	$\frac{1}{2}$ pint	250 ml	$1\frac{1}{4}$ cups
Cooked chicken	8 oz	200 g	$1\frac{1}{2}$ cups
Button mushrooms	2 oz	50 g	$\frac{1}{2}$ cup
Salt and pepper			
Puff pastry	12 oz	300 g	$\frac{3}{4}$ lb
Beaten egg to glaze			

Mix the sauce with the finely-chopped chicken, thinly-sliced mushrooms and seasoning, and leave it to cool. Roll out the pastry 12 × 8 in (30 × 20 cm). Cut it in half across and roll each piece of pastry to a rectangle 12 × 7 in (30 × 17.5 cm). Put one half on a baking tray and pile the chicken filling down the centre. Fold the other piece of pastry in half across the width and use a sharp knife to make cuts on the folded side to within 1 in/2.5 cm of the cut edges. Open out the pastry and place it on top of the chicken filling. Seal the edges with beaten egg and use the egg to glaze the top. Bake at 425°F/220°C/Gas Mark 7 for 40 minutes. Serve hot with vegetables or cold with salad.

Party Chicken Pie

	Imperial	Metric	American
Chicken	3 lb	1.5 kg	3 lb
Carrot	1	1	1
Onion, medium	1	1	1
Bay leaves	2	2	2
Salt			
A few peppercorns			
The chicken liver			
Sliced cooked ham	8 oz	200 g	2 cups
Butter	1½ oz	40 g	3 tbsp
Plain or all-purpose flour	1½ oz	40 g	1½ tbsp
Chicken stock	½ pint	250 ml	1¼ cups
White wine	½ pint	250 ml	1¼ cups
Egg yolk	1	1	1
Single or thin cream	1 tbsp	1 tbsp	1 tbsp
Squeeze of lemon juice			
Chopped parsley	1 tbsp	1 tbsp	1 tbsp
Salt and pepper			
Puff pastry	8 oz	200 g	½ lb
Beaten egg to glaze			

Rinse and wipe the chicken. Place it in a large pan with the carrot, onion, bay leaves, salt, peppercorns, chicken liver and water to cover. Bring to the boil, then simmer for 1–1¼ hours until the chicken is tender. Cool in the liquid for 15 minutes. Lift out the chicken and remove the flesh from the bones. Measure ½ pint/250 ml skimmed and strained chicken stock for the sauce (use the remainder for soup). Cut the ham into cubes. Melt the butter in a saucepan, stir in the flour and remove from the heat. Gradually add the chicken stock, then the wine. Bring to the boil, stirring until the sauce is smooth and thick. Remove from the heat, cool, add the egg yolk, cream, lemon juice, parsley and seasoning to taste. Fill a pie dish with the chicken meat, ham and cooked sauce. Cover it with a pastry lid and decorate with pastry leaves. Leave in the refrigerator to rest for 30 minutes. Brush with beaten egg to glaze. Cook at 450°F/230°C/Gas Mark 8 for 10 minutes. Reduce heat to 400°F/200°C/Gas Mark 6 and continue cooking it for a further 20–25 minutes until the filling is heated through and the pastry golden.

Chicken and Sausage Pie

	Imperial	Metric	American
Pork sausages	8 oz	200 g	$\frac{1}{2}$ lb
Pinch of mixed herbs			
Butter	1 oz	25 g	2 tbsp
Cooked chicken	12 oz	300 g	2 cups
Plain flour	1 oz	25 g	1 tbsp
Chicken stock	$\frac{1}{2}$ pint	250 ml	$1\frac{1}{4}$ cups
Salt and pepper			
Shortcrust pastry	12 oz	300 g	$\frac{3}{4}$ lb
Beaten egg to glaze			

Skin the sausages and mix the meat with the herbs. Form it into 8 balls and fry them in half the butter until golden. Put them in a pie dish with the chopped chicken. Pour off half the fat, add the remaining butter and work in the flour. Blend in the stock and bring it to the boil. Stir well and season to taste. Pour into the pie dish and cool. Cover with the pastry and brush with the beaten egg. Bake at 425°F/220°C/Gas Mark 7 for 40 minutes.

Chicken Flan

	Imperial	Metric	American
Shortcrust pastry	8 oz	200 g	$\frac{1}{2}$ lb
Onion, small	1	1	1
Eating apple	1	1	1
Butter	$\frac{1}{2}$ oz	15 g	1 tbsp
Curry powder	$\frac{1}{2}$ oz	15 g	1 tbsp
Eggs	2	2	2
Milk	$\frac{1}{4}$ pint	125 ml	$\frac{1}{2}$ cup
Salt			
Cooked chicken	6 oz	150 g	1 cup

Roll out the pastry to line an 8-in/12-cm flan ring. Chop the onion and apple and cook them in the butter for 5 minutes over low heat. Add the curry powder and stir it over the heat for 1 minute. Cool the mixture and then mix with the beaten eggs, milk and salt. Cut the chicken into small dice and arrange it in the pastry case. Pour on the curry mixture and bake at 400°F/200°C/Gas Mark 6 for 35 minutes. Serve hot or cold.

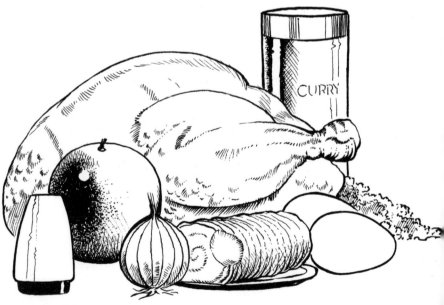

Chicken and Potato Pie

	Imperial	Metric	American
Cooked chicken	1 lb	450 g	3 cups
Potatoes	1 lb	450 g	1 lb
Chicken stock	½ pint	250 ml	1¼ cups
Evaporated milk	½ pint	250 ml	1¼ cups
Salt and pepper			
Chopped parsley	1 tbsp	1 tbsp	1 tbsp
Puff pastry	12 oz	300 g	¾ lb

Cut the chicken and potatoes into small cubes. Mix the stock, evaporated milk, seasoning and parsley and put into a pie dish. Cover with the pastry and bake at 425°F/220°C/Gas Mark 7 for 40 minutes.

Chicken and Cream Cheese Turnover

	Imperial	Metric	American
Cooked chicken	6 oz	150 g	1 cup
Cream cheese	3 oz	75 g	½ cup
Canned pineapple	3 oz	75 g	½ cup
Shortcrust or puff pastry	8 oz	200 g	½ lb
Milk or egg for glazing			

Chop the chicken into small pieces and mix it with the cream cheese and drained chopped pineapple. Roll out the pastry into a large circle and put it on to a baking sheet. Put the chicken mixture on to half the circle. Fold the pastry over to form a turnover and seal the edges. Brush with a little milk or egg to glaze. Bake at 425°F/220°C/Gas Mark 7 for 25 minutes.

Chicken Cobbler

	Imperial	Metric	American
Cooked chicken	12 oz	300 g	$\frac{3}{4}$ lb
Cooked bacon or ham	3 oz	75 g	$\frac{1}{2}$ cup
Condensed mushroom or chicken soup	1 tin	1 tin	1 can
Small packet of frozen peas			
Single or thin cream	4 tbsp	4 tbsp	4 tbsp
Plain or all-purpose flour	8 oz	200 g	8 tbsp
Baking powder	4 tbsp	4 tbsp	4 tsp
Salt	$\frac{1}{2}$ tsp	$\frac{1}{2}$ tsp	$\frac{1}{2}$ tsp
Mustard powder	$\frac{1}{4}$ tsp	$\frac{1}{4}$ tsp	$\frac{1}{4}$ tsp
Curry powder	$\frac{1}{4}$ tsp	$\frac{1}{4}$ tsp	$\frac{1}{4}$ tsp
Butter	2 oz	50 g	4 tbsp
Milk	$\frac{1}{4}$ pint	125 ml	$\frac{1}{2}$ cup
Grated cheese	1 oz	52 g	$\frac{1}{4}$ cup

Pre-heat the oven to 425°F/220°C/Gas Mark 7. Cut the chicken into bite-size pieces and the bacon into smaller pieces. Heat the soup gently in a saucepan, and add the chicken, ham, cooked peas and sufficient cream to give a moist but not liquid consistency. Turn it into a shallow pie dish, spread it evenly and allow to cool while mixing the topping. Sift all the dry ingredients (except the cheese) into a bowl and rub in the fat until the mixture resembles coarse crumbs. Mix to a pliable dough with the milk. On a floured board roll it out to $\frac{1}{2}$-in/1.25-cm thickness and cut out with a 2-in/5-cm round cutter. Arrange the 'biscuits' closely together to cover the entire surface of the pie, brush them lightly with milk and sprinkle with the cheese. Bake in the prepared oven for about 15–30 minutes, reducing the heat to 375°F/190°C/Gas Mark 5 after 10 minutes. The crust should be crisp and golden.

Chapter Eight

CHICKEN SALADS

Everyone loves chicken salad with the accompanying crisp lettuce leaves or tangy fruit in a creamy well-seasoned dressing. To contrast with the white chicken flesh, introduce some colourful vegetables or fruit, or chopped ham. Serve the salad in a glass or wooden bowl, or in individual portions arranged on lettuce leaves. A little chopped parsley or mint, or a sprinkling of chopped nuts makes an attractive finish.

Chicken Salad Veronique

	Imperial	Metric	American
Cooked chicken	12 oz	300 g	2 cups
Green grapes	6 oz	150 g	2 cups
Salad oil	2 tbsp	2 tbsp	2 tbsp
Lemon juice	1 tsp	1 tsp	1 tsp
Grated lemon rind	$\frac{1}{4}$ tsp	$\frac{1}{4}$ tsp	$\frac{1}{4}$ tsp
Salt and pepper			
Single or thin cream	4 tbsp	4 tbsp	4 tbsp
Crisp lettuce leaves			
Tomatoes	2	2	2

Cut the chicken into bite-size pieces and mix with the halved and de-seeded grapes. Combine the oil, lemon juice and rind, seasonings and cream; then stir this dressing into the chicken and grape mixture. Cover it and set aside in a refrigerator to allow the flavours to blend. To serve, line a shallow bowl with lettuce leaves, pile the chicken salad into the centre and garnish with thin wedges of tomato.

Summer Salad

	Imperial	Metric	American
Long-grain rice	4 oz	100 g	$\frac{2}{3}$ cup
Cooked peas	4 oz	100 g	1 cup
French dressing			
Cooked chicken portions	4	4	4
Lettuce			
Fresh grapefruit sections			
Cherries or strawberries	4 oz	100 g	1 cup
Black grapes	4 oz	100 g	1 cup
Peaches	2	2	2
Feather Cream Dressing			
Egg white	1	1	1
Commercial soured cream or sour cream	$\frac{1}{4}$ pint	125 ml	$\frac{1}{2}$ cup
Good mayonnaise	$\frac{1}{4}$ pint	125 ml	$\frac{1}{2}$ cup
Salt			
Paprika	2 tsp	2 tsp	2 tsp

Cook and drain the rice, and add the peas and
enough French dressing to moisten. Pile it into the
centre of a dish and chill. Take portions of chicken,
each in one piece, such as drumsticks, or thighs with
bone removed, or whole or half chicken breasts.
Arrange them on the rice. Surround them with crisp
lettuce leaves and fill these with the fruits. Make the
dressing by whisking the egg white until very stiff and
folding in the cream, mayonnaise, salt and paprika.
If possible, make it in advance so that the paprika
will colour the dressing a delicate pink. Use a little
to coat the chicken and serve the rest in a sauceboat.

Sunshine Salad

	Imperial	Metric	American
Mayonnaise	4 tbsp	4 tbsp	4 tbsp
Bottled sauce	1 tbsp	1 tbsp	1 tbsp
Double or thick cream	¼ pint	125 ml	½ cup
Cooked chicken	12 oz	300 g	2 cups
Orange	1	1	1
Eating apple	1	1	1
Cucumber	2 in	5 cm	2 in
Spring onion	1	1	1
Salt and pepper			
Lettuce leaves	4	4	4

Mix the mayonnaise and sauce. Whip the cream to soft peaks and mix in the mayonnaise mixture. Chop the chicken into neat dice. Peel the orange and divide it into segments. Do not peel the apple, but cut it in quarters, remove the core and cut the apple into neat slices. Dice the cucumber and slice the spring onion. Mix the chicken, orange, apple, cucumber and onion into the cream and season with salt and pepper to taste. Arrange 4 portions on lettuce leaves on individual plates.

Spring Salad

	Imperial	Metric	American
Long-grain rice	6 oz	150 g	1 cup
Small packet frozen peas or mixed vegetables	1	1	1
Sultanas	2 oz	50 g	$\frac{1}{2}$ cup
Cooked chicken	12 oz	300 g	2 cups
Salad cream	6 tbsp	6 tbsp	6 tbsp
Top of the milk	4 tbsp	4 tbsp	4 tbsp
Curry powder	$\frac{1}{4}$ tsp	$\frac{1}{4}$ tsp	$\frac{1}{4}$ tsp
Salt	$\frac{1}{2}$ tsp	$\frac{1}{2}$ tsp	$\frac{1}{2}$ tsp
Watercress			
Tomatoes			

Boil a pan of salted water and add the rice. Cook it for 5 minutes, then add the vegetables and sultanas and cook for 7 minutes. Drain it and leave to cool. Chop the chicken into neat pieces and mix with the rice and vegetables. Mix the salad cream, milk, curry powder and salt and pour it over the rice mixture. Stir thoroughly and put into a salad bowl. Garnish with watercress and tomato wedges.

Chicken Salad Caprice

	Imperial	Metric	American
Large ripe banana	1	1	1
Lemon juice	2 tbsp	2 tbsp	2 tbsp
Large orange	1	1	1
Cooked chicken	12 oz	300 g	2 cups
Mayonnaise	3 tbsp	3 tbsp	3 tbsp
Cream	2 tbsp	2 tbsp	2 tbsp
Crisp lettuce leaves			
Black grapes	4 oz	100 g	1 cup

Slice the banana into a bowl and turn it over and over in the lemon juice. Peel the orange and add the segments, freed from skin and pips, to the bowl. Add the chicken cut into ½-in (1.25-cm) dice, the mayonnaise and the cream. Mix together lightly, cover, and set aside in a refrigerator to allow the flavours to blend. To serve, line a shallow bowl with lettuce leaves, pile the chicken salad in the centre and garnish with the halved and de-seeded grapes.

Virginia Chicken Salad

	Imperial	Metric	American
Medium dessert apples	2	2	2
Lemon juice	3 tbsp	3 tbsp	3 tbsp
Double or thick cream	4 tbsp	4 tbsp	4 tbsp
Salad cream	2 tbsp	2 tbsp	2 tbsp
Salt	¼ tsp	¼ tsp	¼ tsp
Cooked chicken	8 oz	200 g	1½ cups
Sticks or stalks of celery	4	4	4
Walnuts	1 tbsp	1 tbsp	1 tbsp
Crisp lettuce leaves			
Small red-skinned apple	1	1	1
Sprigs of parsley			

Peel and core the apples, cut them into dice and toss with 1 tbsp lemon juice. Lightly whip the cream and stir into it the salad cream, salt and 1 tbsp lemon juice. Add the diced apple, chicken, celery and nuts. Mix, cover and set aside in a refrigerator. To serve, arrange the lettuce leaves around a flat dish and pile the chicken salad in the centre. Cut the unpeeled red-skinned apple into slices and dip them in the remaining lemon juice. Garnish the salad with the apple slices and parsley sprigs.

Danish Chicken Cocktail

	Imperial	Metric	American
Cooked chicken	12 oz	300 g	2 cups
Mayonnaise	½ pint	250 ml	1¼ cups
Tomato sauce	2 tbsp	2 tbsp	2 tbsp
Lemon juice	2 tbsp	2 tbsp	2 tbsp
Worcestershire sauce	1 tsp	1 tsp	1 tsp
Curry powder	1 tsp	1 tsp	1 tsp
Salt and pepper			
Small lettuce	1	1	1
Cucumber	¼	¼	¼
Tomato	1	1	1

Cut the chicken into neat strips. Mix the
mayonnaise with tomato sauce, lemon juice,
Worcestershire sauce, curry powder, salt and pepper.
Stir in the chicken carefully. Shred the lettuce very
finely and dice the cucumber, leaving the skin on.
Mix the lettuce and cucumber and arrange in four
individual bowls or glasses. Pile the chicken mayonnaise
on top and garnish with the tomato cut in quarters.

Chicken and Chestnut Salad

	Imperial	Metric	American
Cooked chicken	8 oz	200 g	1½ cups
Cooked chestnuts	4 oz	100 g	1 cup
Sticks or stalks of celery	2	2	2
Hard-boiled eggs	2	2	2
Spanish stuffed olives	8	8	8
Mayonnaise	½ pint	250 ml	1¼ cups
Lettuce leaves			
Watercress			

Chop the chicken in small pieces, and chop the chestnuts and celery. Slice the eggs and olives. Mix the chicken, chestnuts, celery, eggs and olives carefully in the mayonnaise. Arrange on lettuce leaves and garnish with watercress. This is a good dish just after Christmas when chestnuts are easily available.

Chicken and Pineapple Salad

	Imperial	Metric	American
Canned pineapple	6 oz	150 g	medium can
Salad oil	1 tbsp	1 tbsp	1 tbsp
Lemon juice	1 tbsp	1 tbsp	1 tbsp
Finely-grated lemon rind	$\frac{1}{4}$ tsp	$\frac{1}{4}$ tsp	$\frac{1}{4}$ tsp
Pineapple juice	2 tbsp	2 tbsp	2 tbsp
Salt	$\frac{1}{4}$ tsp	$\frac{1}{4}$ tsp	$\frac{1}{4}$ tsp
Cooked chicken	12 oz	300 g	2 cups
Chopped mint	1 tsp	1 tsp	1 tsp
Crisp lettuce leaves	8	8	8
Watercress			

Drain the pineapple pieces and chop them finely. Prepare the dressing in a large basin by mixing together the oil, lemon juice and rind, pineapple juice and salt. Add the chicken, cut into dice, and the pineapple pieces. Cover and set it aside in a refrigerator to allow the flavours to blend. Shortly before serving stir in the chopped mint and divide the salad among the cupped lettuce leaves. Arrange around a flat serving dish and garnish the centre with a small bunch of watercress.

Chicken and Cucumber Salad

	Imperial	Metric	American
Cucumber, large	1	1	1
Cooked chicken	12 oz	300 g	2 cups
Single or thin cream	2 tbsp	2 tbsp	2 tbsp
Mayonnaise	2 tbsp	2 tbsp	2 tbsp
Lemon juice	2 tsp	2 tsp	2 tsp
Chopped mint	1 tsp	1 tsp	1 tsp
Salt			
Tomatoes	2	2	2
Hard-boiled egg	1	1	1

Cut the cucumber in half. Thinly slice one half, and cut the other half into small cubes. Cut the chicken into small pieces. Prepare the dressing by mixing cream, mayonnaise, lemon juice, mint and salt together, and then stir in the chopped cucumber and chicken. Set aside in a cool place for an hour for the flavours to blend. When ready to serve, pile the chicken in the centre of a flat dish, circle it with cucumber slices and garnish with sliced tomato and hard-boiled egg.

Gourmet Chicken Salad

	Imperial	Metric	American
Thick portions cooked chicken	4	4	4
Mayonnaise	4 tbsp	4 tbsp	4 tbsp
Thick cream	2 tbsp	2 tbsp	2 tbsp
Lemon juice	2 tsp	2 tsp	2 tsp
Paprika			

	Imperial	Metric	American
Tomatoes	4	4	4
Cucumber	$\frac{1}{2}$	$\frac{1}{2}$	$\frac{1}{2}$
Cress			

Keeping the portions as whole as possible, remove the skin and bones and arrange the portions down the centre of a flat serving dish. Mix together the mayonnaise, cream and lemon juice, and spoon it over the chicken to form a thick coating. Decorate each portion with a light sprinkling of paprika. Skin the tomatoes and cut them into thin slices. Slice the cucumber. Arrange alternating slices of tomato and cucumber all around the dish and garnish with cress.

Crunchy Summer Salad

	Imperial	Metric	American
Cooked chicken	1 lb	450 g	3 cups
Hard-boiled eggs	2	2	2
Spanish stuffed green olives	12	12	12
Green pepper	1	1	1
Tomatoes	3	3	3
Cauliflower	8 oz	200 g	2 cups
Small lettuce	1	1	1
Olive oil	$\frac{1}{4}$ pint	125 ml	$\frac{1}{2}$ cup
Lemon juice	4 tbsp	4 tbsp	4 tbsp
Chopped fresh mint	1 tsp	1 tsp	1 tsp
Salt and pepper			

Cut the chicken into match-stick pieces. Slice the eggs, green pepper and skinned tomatoes. Break the raw cauliflower into small pieces and shred the lettuce. Mix the oil, lemon juice, mint and seasoning, and leave it to stand for 1 hour. Put all the salad ingredients into a serving bowl. Slice olives and add to salad. Mix the dressing well, pour it over the salad, and toss it lightly.

Chapter Nine

LEFTOVER CHICKEN

A little leftover chicken makes a marvellous second-day dish. There need be no waste, for chicken meat is lean all through. Use minced chicken to make croquettes, patties or a mousse, or chop the chicken to use in sandwiches, pancakes or vol-au-vent cases. If the chicken carcass is simmered in water to make stock, this liquid will give added flavour to second-day dishes and can be used also as the basis of delicious and nourishing soups.

Chicken Pancakes

	Imperial	Metric	American
Plain or all-purpose flour	4 oz	100 g	8 tbsp
Pinch of salt			
Egg	1	1	1
Milk	½ pint	250 ml	1¼ cups
Cooked chicken	8 oz	200 g	1½ cups
Cooked peas	8 oz	200 g	1½ cups
Condensed chicken soup	1	1	1
Salt and pepper			

Sift the flour and salt into a basin. Add the egg and half the milk and beat well until smooth. Add the rest of the milk. Lightly grease a frying pan and cook thin pancakes with the batter. Cut the chicken into small dice and mix with the peas and soup. Season well. Put a little chicken mixture in the centre of each pancake, roll up and arrange in a greased ovenware dish. Heat at 350°F/180°C/Gas Mark 4 for 20 minutes.

Danish Chicken Soup

	Imperial	Metric	American
Chicken stock	2 pints	1 l	5 cups
Eggs	2	2	2
Curry powder	2 tsp	2 tsp	2 tsp

Heat the stock to boiling point. Beat the eggs and curry powder with a fork and add to the hot stock, stirring carefully with a fork. Serve at once.

Chicken Patties

	Imperial	Metric	American
Cooked chicken	12 oz	300 g	2 cups
Cooked bacon or ham	4 oz	100 g	1 cup
Small onion	1	1	1
Salt and pepper			
Pinch of nutmeg			
Chopped parsley	1 tbsp	1 tbsp	1 tbsp
White sauce	½ pint	250 ml	1¼ cups
Egg yolk	1	1	1
Flour			
Beaten egg			
Bread crumbs			

Mince together the chicken, bacon or ham, and onion. Season well with salt, pepper, nutmeg and parsley and mix it with the white sauce and egg yolk. Mix well and then divide into 8 pieces. Form into patties, dip in flour, then in beaten egg and breadcrumbs. Leave them in a cold place for 20 minutes, then fry in hot fat. Eat hot or cold with vegetables or salad, or use them to fill buttered crusty rolls.

Chicken Croquettes

	Imperial	Metric	American
Cooked chicken	12 oz	300 g	2 cups
Butter	1 oz	25 g	2 tbsp
Plain or all-purpose flour	1 oz	25 g	1 tbsp
Chicken stock or milk	$\frac{1}{4}$ pint	125 ml	$\frac{1}{2}$ cup
Mushrooms	2 oz	50 g	$\frac{1}{2}$ cup
Chopped parsley	1 tsp	1 tsp	1 tsp
Salt and pepper			
Egg	1	1	1
Breadcrumbs			
Fat for frying			

Mince the chicken finely. Melt the butter, blend in the flour and stock or milk gradually, and stir well over low heat. Add the chopped mushrooms and parsley and cook for 3 minutes. Season well and stir in the chicken, mixing well. Turn on to a plate to cool. Cut into 16 equal-sized pieces and roll into sausage shapes. Coat the croquettes with beaten egg and breadcrumbs and fry them in hot fat until golden and hot right through.

Leek and Potato Soup

	Imperial	Metric	American
Small onion	1	1	1
Medium leeks	4	4	4
Medium potatoes	3	3	3
Butter	2 oz	50 g	4 tbsp
Chicken stock	2 pints	1 l	5 cups
Salt and pepper			
Single or thin cream	2 tbsp	2 tbsp	2 tbsp

Chop the onion finely. Clean the leeks well
and cut them into rings. Peel and dice the potatoes.
Melt the butter and cook the vegetables over low heat
for 5 minutes. Add the stock and season well. Cover
and simmer for 45 minutes until the vegetables are
soft. Stir in the cream and serve hot. If preferred, the
soup may be sieved or liquidized before adding the
cream. If the smooth soup is chilled and sprinkled with
chopped fresh chives, it becomes the popular Vichyssoise.

Fried Chicken Sandwiches

	Imperial	Metric	American
Cooked chicken	12 oz	300 g	2 cups
Salt and pepper			
Pinch of nutmeg			
Chopped parsley	1 tsp	1 tsp	1 tsp
White sauce	6 tbsp	6 tbsp	6 tbsp
Egg yolk	1	1	1
Bread slices	8	8	8
Milk	½ pint	250 ml	1¼ cups
Eggs	2	2	2
Breadcrumbs			
Oil for frying			

Mince the chicken and mix it with salt, pepper,
nutmeg, parsley, white sauce and egg yolk. Make
sandwiches with this mixture and cut each in half.
Beat together the milk, eggs and a little salt and
pepper. Dip the chicken sandwiches into this, coat
them with breadcrumbs and fry in hot oil until
golden. Medium-thick bread slices are best for
sandwiches. Serve with salad or pickles.

Chicken Mousse

	Imperial	Metric	American
Cooked chicken	8 oz	200 g	1½ cups
Chicken stock	½ pint	250 ml	1¼ cups
Gelatine	¼ oz	7 g	½ tbsp
Double or thick cream	¼ pint	125 ml	½ cup
Salt and pepper			
Cucumber and tomato			

Mince the chicken twice using the smallest cutter. Crush the chicken carcass, add vegetables and herbs for flavouring, barely cover with water and simmer for about 1 hour. Strain the stock and reduce it to ½ pint/250 ml. Dissolve the gelatine in the stock and add half to the chicken meat. Whisk the cream until fluffy but not stiff. Fold in the chicken and seasonings. Transfer it to a glass dish and chill until set. Pour half the remaining jellied stock on top. Arrange a simple decoration of cucumber and tomato and then cover it with the rest of the stock. Chill before serving with a green salad.

Victorian Chicken Toasts

	Imperial	Metric	American
White sauce	½ pint	250 ml	1¼ cups
Cooked chicken	12 oz	300 g	2 cups
Small onion	1	1	1
Butter	1 oz	25 g	2 tbsp
Cooked potato	8 oz	200 g	1½ cups
Toast slices, Chopped chives			

If possible, make the white sauce with chicken stock, and then stir in the diced chicken. Chop the onion very finely and cook it in the butter until soft and golden. Stir the onion and diced potato into the chicken mixture and heat through. Serve hot on toast, sprinkled with chopped chives.

INDEX